The Old Testament
as
Word of God

The Old Testament as Word of God

SIGMUND MOWINCKEL
Translated by Reidar B. Bjornard

Abingdon Press
New York • Nashville

THE OLD TESTAMENT AS WORD OF GOD

Translated from *Det Gamle Testament som Guds Ord*
Gyldendal Norsk Forlag, Oslo, 1938

Library of Congress Catalog Card Number: 59-10365

SET UP, PRINTED, AND BOUND BY THE
PARTHENON PRESS, AT NASHVILLE,
TENNESSEE, UNITED STATES OF AMERICA

Foreword

This book records a series of lectures for a nontheological audience in 1938. It was brought about by a practical need for information about problems which were quite elementary theologically speaking. These were felt by newly awakened lay people of all classes, but mostly by the more educated ones among them. Especially the Old Testament caused many questions to be raised, and they can be summed up in the title of this book: How can the many apparent or real obscurities in the Old Testament be harmonized with the assertion that it is word of God? Many frank conversations with my friends made it clear to me that they needed help not only to view the Old Testament as history, but also to grasp the dimension of revelation in that history.

The problems and needs today are largely the same as twenty years ago. They are independent of the shifting currents and interests which move within technical theology. The problems are elementary from a theological standpoint, but to the faith and the thoughtful believer they are important and vital. According to my experience we need to carry on an open conversation, to attempt to see the Old Testament as it really is and as God has given it to us and not to view it veiled by pedantic verbalisms or through dogmatic glasses. We are not here primarily interested in the scientific tenability of any one of the critical hypotheses, indispensable as these may be for a complete theological study. We are rather looking for the basic viewpoint, the historical view of the Bible.

These considerations give me the courage to allow the book to appear in English translation without great changes over twenty years after it was first published. I hope that it may be of some use also in its new form.

A few smaller additions have been made to the Norwegian text, and in the footnotes newer literature in English has been included. The notes, however, only will direct the attention to a few sources where the interested reader may find more information. The popular aim of the book has limited the number of notes to a minimum.

I here express my deep gratitude to the translator, my past student, Professor Reidar B. Bjornard, for his proposal to have the book translated and for the work he has done on it. Likewise I thank the Abingdon Press for the publication of the book and for the format they have given to it.

SIGMUND MOWINCKEL

Contents

1. The discussion of the subject of this book is mostly of a popular nature. It is of course relevant to the areas of systematic thought, but it makes no claim to be advanced systematic thinking. The viewpoints that I try to give are attempts to arrive at a view of the Old Testament that is practical in the service of the religious life. This is done by taking up various topics and letting light fall on them from various angles.

Now and again it is profitable to take time to rethink the elementary things in our spiritual heritage, as well as that which is elementary in our Christian thinking. By elementary I mean what comes to mind immediately from our observation of reality and from relationship with it. This precedes advanced systematization, and our thinking again and again has to return to this immediate observation of reality.

The Old Testament—Word of God

2. The Church meets man with the message that *the Old Testament is Word of God,* and the whole New Testament is built upon this judgment. Both for Jesus and for the apostles the Old Testament was "the holy Scripture." It is by referring to the Old Testament that Jesus answers questions from others about true fear of God, true life, true understanding of God, and also about the difficulties of his own human life, temptation, and distress. With the Old Testament he resists Satan, and from the Old Testament he finds clarification of his calling, and comfort in his temptations and sufferings. "According to the Scriptures this had to happen to the Son of man."

Again, it was in the light of the Old Testament that the apostles understood who Jesus was and what his life's work meant. The Old Testament gave them the interpretation of the suffering and atoning Servant of the Lord instead of the Jewish Messiah.

But how should the fact that the Old Testament was Word of God be explained? Here, we no longer have merely an immediate observation of religious reality, but an attempt on the part of human thought to understand and to achieve order in its spiritual inheritance. To this question the apostles could obtain only that answer of which their time was capable. It naturally was the one that contemporary Judaism offered: namely, that Scripture in one way or another is "inspired by God," dictated word for word, so to speak, by a mystical, divine act. This perhaps is illustrated best, not by an abstract formulation of opinion, but by the picture of "inspiration" that is rendered in II Esdras 14:37 ff.:

> "Ezra, open your mouth and drink what I give you to drink." Then I opened my mouth, and behold, a full cup was offered to me; it was full of something like water, but its color was like fire. And I took it and drank; and when I had drunk it, my heart poured forth understanding, and wisdom increased in my breast, for my spirit retained its memory; and my mouth was opened, and was no longer closed.

Aside from this more mystical concept we can find another more rationalistic, or rather a mythological-rationalistic, theory: namely, that "the Law" was written by God himself and was pre-existent in heaven, and from there it was dictated to Moses "mouth to mouth." This opinion was also related to the idea that God or the Spirit had dictated to the prophets through visionary experiences what they were to tell about the future and the last things. As inspired by God, the Scriptures were "profitable for teaching, for reproof, for correction, and for training in righteousness." It was necessary to obey them.

As time passed, countless *Christians* found God's word for themselves in the Old Testament. For the teaching of the *Church* and the practice of believers the Old Testament and the New Testament form a unity—"the holy Scripture," "the Word of God." This belief is the presupposition for the following reflections, and they are written in the belief that in the Old Testament we really do have word of God, and they are also written for those who share this faith. They are written, finally, because this belief raises a problem for our thinking and for our reading of the Bible.

3. The Church has developed this theory in a way which seems to contradict reality. The Jewish view, as we see it in II Esdras and as it is taken over by II Timothy, is still not a pure, intellectual theory. It rather has the character of an immediate, practical, religious experience and evaluation, still seeking an appropriate form of expression in thought. In one place, for example, it employs a picture, as in II Esdras, and in another is satisfied with a simple reference to the spirit of God, as is common in apocalyptic writings, the wisdom literature, and rabbinic lore. Or it may sometimes be expressed in general terms as "inspiration" from God, as in early Christianity (II Timothy). It is on this rather nontheoretical level that the Roman Catholic Church, in the main, has stood.

The sharpest formulation of the idea was given by the early Lutheran theologians in the "theory of verbal inspiration," which was applied to the Old and New Testaments without differentiation. The Scripture was created by divine inspiration that had the character of direct divine dictation. The Holy Spirit told the authors both the content and the form of that which they wrote. Scripture therefore, it was held, was "infallible" even in externals and down to the smallest details. It contained historical, geographical, botanical, zoological, and metaphysical "information about reality," as if for the sake of this information itself. In Gen. 1, for instance, it was the purpose of God to inform us about the time sequence of creation and how the universe was put in order.

In reality this early Lutheran theory is only an elaboration of the Jewish-rabbinical theory. There is probably also a historical connection between the two and not merely an analogy between the two points of view.

The Old Testament—A Human Book

4. The teaching of the Church and the experience of religious people with the Old Testament as word of God, however, raise a *problem* that is met by the theological student at the outset of his study. The teaching of the Church and this judgment of religious people about the Old Testament *seem* to contradict the results of a realistic study of the Old Testament itself. It is the factual nature and the content of the Old Testament that create the issue.

One cannot close one's eyes to the fact that the Old Testament contains many statements of historical, geographical, chronological, and biological nature, and so on, that simply cannot be harmonized with the present stage of our knowledge, statements which, therefore, to that extent are *erroneous*.

As examples one can mention the *chronology* in the Books of Moses, which dates creation at about four thousand years before Christ. Geology and archaeology and the historical records, however, agree that the history of the earth and mankind is much older. Around 4,000 B.C., for instance, there was a high culture in Babylonia, Egypt, India, and China; and it must have taken millenniums to develop. Again, geology and paleontology show that the earth with its vegetable and animal life goes back millions of years.

Or to take another detail: The Old Testament tells us that it was the Assyrian King Shalmaneser V who in 722 B.C. took Samaria (II Kings 18:9-10). But contemporary Assyrian documents show that the city was taken by Sargon II, the successor of Shalmaneser V. In the Old Testament the hare also is counted among the animals who chew the cud (Deut. 14:7), and no apologetic art has succeeded in justifying this classification.

5. It is not necessary, however, to hinge upon such details. More important is the fact that closer investigation will prove how the Old Testament in all points *is related to the culture, mentality, morality, and knowledge of a specific time,* and in many ways reflects the characteristically Jewish view of life, God, and man.[1] This Israelitic-Jewish way of thinking about ethics and culture, in turn, stands in close relationship to the whole ancient Oriental culture and mentality. It is a way of thought and feeling, of evaluation and expression, which in many ways is foreign to us and our Christian view with its western ethics and value judgments. It is, therefore, difficult for us to grasp. A comparative study of religion and culture will show that in decisive points it belongs to so-called "primitive" mentality. By the word "primitive" no derogative value judgment is intended, but simply the recognition of a view of life and reality that is wholly different from the modern scientific

[1] The reader will find a good description of the nature of Hebrew literature in general and the origin and date of the single books of the Old Testament in Aage Bentzen, *Introduction to the Old Testament* (2nd ed.; Copenhagen: E. C. Gad, 1953).

view, the two pillars of which are the rational thinking of the Greeks and the Christian evaluation of man.

Once one has seen this, then one also cannot escape seeing that much of the specifically Old Testament material lies *below the Christian level* as given both in the New Testament and in the modern ideals of humanity, all of which derive their concrete content from Christianity.

One can notice the nationalistic limitation of religion in the Old Testament: namely, that Yahweh (as the Deity was called) is—in spite of the work of the prophets—always primarily the God for Israel and the Jews, and seems to maintain the cause of his people even when they are in the wrong. Even those views about the last days and final salvation in "Deutero-Isaiah" (Isa. 40 ff.), which are the most universalistic in nature within the Old Testament, make salvation a matter for the Jews first. The other nations share in it only to the extent that they humble themselves and become Jews, or become their downright political, social, and economic vassals.[2]

Similar to this is the religious motivation of hatred against national enemies: Yahweh "loved Jacob [that is, the Jews] but . . . hated Esau [that is, the Edomites and the other neighboring nations]." Consider also the burning prayers in the Psalms for revenge over national and personal enemies.

The religious sanctioning and regulating of an obligation to carry out the vendetta testify to both a primitive state of life and a sub-Christian morality that is just beginning to be aware of the difference between intentional and unintentional crime. The same is true of the rigid principle of retaliation "An eye for an eye and a tooth for a tooth." One can say, as a whole, that

[2] See, for instance, Isa. 45:14-17; 60:4 ff.; Mic. 4:1-5; Zech. 14:12-19.

the Old Testament view of punishment and its purpose contradicts Christian and humane principles: The purpose of "the Law of Moses" was never the improvement and education of the lawbreaker but only retaliation and prevention, as expressed in the saying "You shall purge the evil from Israel." It was not until the prophets that the idea of God's punishment as a warning and educative discipline began to appear. And just as revenge and retaliation have clear religious sanction in the Old Testament, so also have slavery, polygamy, different standards of sexual morality for man and woman, different treatment of members and nonmembers of the religious society. "You shall not lend upon interest to your brother . . . . To a foreigner you may lend upon interest." (Deut. 23:19, 20.)

6. If one continues on the road of impartial research and renounces all more or less dishonest efforts to explain away the embarrassing passages (which always have been so typical of theology), then one soon will find that the Old Testament is not a homogeneous entity with everything on one plane and in complete harmony. Some examples may be cited: The "Law of Moses" demands that only one place shall be the legal place for worship and sacrifice in Israel (namely, Jerusalem), and the author of the books of Kings judges all previous kings and leaders according to whether they kept or broke this law. On the other hand, the patriarchal stories in Genesis and a series of the old stories, which the books of Kings themselves have recorded, show that in the whole of antiquity this was not so. Right down to the fall of Judah (587 B.C.) there were, in fact, several holy places around the country, and they were looked upon by all the leading religious men, whether priests or prophets, as legal and as founded by Yahweh himself. That there ever had been a law to the contrary, none of them appears to be aware, not even the stern prophets of doom. A closer look at the Law itself will reveal two views. One law about altars and holy places unequivocally presupposes, like the older traditions, that there exist and shall exist many such sanctioned places (Exod. 20:24-26). Other passages, however (Deut. 12 ff.), under threat of the death penalty forbid all other places of sacrifice except the one (in Jerusalem). Even about this single place the opinions are varied: some books and passages in the Old Testament consider the many places to be "lawful," inaugurated or at least sanctioned by God during the time before Solomon built his Temple in Jerusalem (Deuteronomy and the author of the book of Kings). Other books, however (the Chronicles and the so-called "P" passages of the Law, especially Leviticus), maintain that there had always been only one legal sanctuary, even in the time of the patriarchs and the desert wanderings, namely, that of a portable holy tent that was instituted by Moses ("The Tabernacle").

Against the particularistic national religion and the externalizing sacrificial religion, the great prophets of doom—Amos, Hosea, Isaiah, Micah, Zephaniah, and Jeremiah—raised a flaming protest. They rejected both the idea that Israel was preferred to the other nations and the idea that the sacrifice was well-pleasing to God, and this in spite of all "holy" tradition in Israel in their own day. Between "the Law" and "the Prophets" there is a huge cleft, an essential difference. The sovereignty of "the Law" in later Judaism really means that now the universalistic and spiritualizing tendencies of the prophets have been strangled or deflected, accepted in form but blunted in reality; the prophets are killed and their graves adorned (cf. Luke 11:47). It means that both nationalistic particularism and external worship have won out again. These tendencies triumph both in "the Law" and in the compilations and editions of the Prophets. For the prophetic books, as we have them today, are really sayings of the prophets worked over by the Jews.

This heterogeneity extends also to less important things and to details. The Creation is given, as is well known, in two quite different stories. The one (Gen. 1) lets the earth emerge from the ocean and says that man was created after the animals. The other (Gen. 2) says that before the rise of the world there was only desert, that creation started by God's allowing it to rain, and that man was created before the animals. Concerning the rise of the kingdom in Israel, one story (I Sam. 9) says that it was Yahweh himself who decided the matter in order to give Israel a savior from its enemies, the Philistines, and that he ordered Samuel to anoint Saul. Another story (I Sam. 8 and 10) says that it was something that the people contrived in discontent and distrust and against the will of Yahweh and against the most earnest advice of Samuel. In the first story the kingdom is a gift of God, in the second a result of human sin and pride. The opinions in the Old Testament are also divided about the Ten Commandments given at Sinai. Exod. 20 and Deut. 5 say that the Ten Commandments were the familiar ten that we have in our Lutheran catechism, but in Exod. 34 it is quite another decalogue that is the foundation of the covenant at Sinai. Only three of the commandments are the same. The former ten commandments are predominantly social-ethical, whereas the latter are more cultic-ritualistic.

7. If we study the leading *religious personalities* in the Old Testament, the prophets, we find here also strong *individual differences* in style and language, temper and poetic ability, and in the content of their ethical preaching and the total view undergirding it. Between the concise figurative style of Isaiah (1–39) and the broad rhetorical and lyrically swelling, hymn-like sayings of "Deutero-Isaiah" (Isa. 40–66) there is an almost absolute difference. Against the merciless harshness in the word of judgment as it was preached by the great prophets of doom and their apparently emotionless identification with the hard word of God that they proclaim, one will recall the touching testimonies about the personal sufferings that the word of doom caused a man like Jeremiah, who constantly seems to vacillate between an identification with the word of doom and an identification with his own people against that word. Behind the prophetic words introduced by the authoritative "Thus sayeth Yahweh" we can see more or less clearly the *man* Isaiah, the *man* Jeremiah, and their individual natures, relationships, and circumstances.

This *human* nature appears in the Old Testament in another way also. In the Psalms we have expressions of man's distress and lament, longing, prayer and fear of God, doubt, hope and faith, trust, joy, thanksgiving and adoration. If anything, *prayer* is man's innermost personal affair. That prayer also is "word of God" is something to which we will return later.

Briefly then, the Old Testament is not a homogeneous entity, not something closed and completed, as we might instinctively expect the "Word of God" to be. On the contrary, it bears the clear marks of a diverse human history with many cross-current lines. Or in other words, the Old Testament appears to us as a very human book.[3]

[3] J. A. Montgomery, *The Bible, the Book of God and of Man* (Ventnor City, N. J.: Ventnor Publs., 1948), pp. 24 ff., 31 ff.

8. With this insight we have arrived at the problem of the Old Testament for theology—that is, for Christian thought, Christian preaching, and Christian reading of the Bible. The word of God in the Old Testament proves to be human words. Is there here an irreconcilable contradiction, an either-or? Or can the two sides really be seen as two sides of the same thing? Can the apparent contradictions be united?

The conviction that the Old Testament contains the revelation of God is certainly one that the Church cannot give up without compelling reasons. For it builds upon the authority of Jesus and the apostles, upon the Church's knowledge of the truth (which, according to the promise of Jesus, would be guided by the Holy Spirit), and upon the experience of the believers.

How then can the Old Testament be divine revelation and at the same time a very human book, characterized by human imperfection and weakness, by specific circumstances of specific men and peoples and periods, spoken and written out of their midst and addressed to them; an absolute and at the same time a relative entity; a human work and at the same time an inspired book? To use the words of Hempel,[4] the problem is "whether a religion, with a stamp so characteristic of its own time and place, being bound by thousands of threads to the past and to the environment formed by the Semitic-Oriental religions, can claim to be a religion of revelation." We may also formulate the problem in this way: The religion of the Old Testament is a historical entity with all the conditioning and limitation that pertain thereto. How can it also be an eternal entity, the beginning of the kingdom of God?

[4] J. Hempel, *Altes Testament und Geschichte* (Gütersloh: C. Bertelsmann, 1930).

The Presupposition for the Solution of the Problem

9. First it must be emphasized that the *presupposition* for the existence of the problem and for the possibility of its solution is that one start from a positive *Christian standpoint.* The problem simply does not exist for one whose standpoint is non-Christian, atheistic, or agnostic; for such a standpoint no such thing as a revelation of God exists. Neither can the solution of the problem, therefore, be made a condition for accepting the Christian standpoint, or Christianity itself. It simply cannot be solved until, for other reasons, one has found and adopted a Christian standpoint. One cannot wait to adopt an attitude toward God until one has gained clarity in the problem of scripture and inspiration. It is clarity in one's relationship to God, that is, a conscious willingness created by God to belong to God and to receive him and his grace and power as he really gives them and as one really needs them, and God's active answer to this willingness, which gives and creates both faith and understanding. Seek first the kingdom of God, then come and receive clarity in theological-religious intellectual problems, Jesus would say.

The presupposition for the solution of the problem is that we acknowledge that a reality called the revelation of God exists, that something designated by the term "inspiration" or "inspired word" exists as a real thing.

Beyond this it may be practical to distinguish between the two words "revelation" and "inspiration." *Revelation* means (1) that God imparts himself to us and (2) the content of that which he thus imparts or gives. *Inspiration* means (1) that God puts man into a position to receive and grasp that which he reveals and to pass it on; it is, then, also (2) the condition of mind, the specific mental equipment and activity, through which God imparts himself.

Theory of Inspiration and Reality of Revelation

10. First we have to notice that what is said above about the actual nature of the Old Testament does not in reality conflict with the belief that it contains the revelation of God and is inspired word and writing. That with which it does conflict and which makes the problem apparently insoluble is the conventional *theory* of inspiration, that is, verbal inspiration and its modern regalvanization, "fundamentalism," that does not permit a judgment that the "revelation of God" contains "errors" and historically conditioned relativity. Thus it is our *human concepts* that make the problem difficult.

The *doctrine* of verbal inspiration is not in the Bible in reality. The statement that "all scripture is inspired by God" is an erroneous translation. The correct rendering undoubtedly is: "Every scripture inspired by God is useful for doctrine" (II Tim. 3:16). It is often written that God said such and such, yes, even that an angel or the Spirit "dictated" this or that. But nowhere is it said that this pertains to the whole mass of writings, word for word and letter for letter. Quite the contrary! Luke says that he will write his Gospel because none of the previous ones was satisfactory. Among these, however, was the Gospel according to Mark. But aside from this, even if the Bible said that the Scriptures in their totality and their several parts, as books, were inspired by God—and this is what we really believe!—the teaching of literal infallibility is *not* contained in the doctrine of inspiration. It is an arbitrary conclusion drawn by over-clever theologians, first Jews and later Christians, from biblical thought about the inspired words and writings. It is twisted theological deduction, an impermissible use of formal logic, nothing more.

11. Behind the theory, however, there is a reality and an experience: the *reality that God has revealed himself* and *inspired* his witnesses, and the *experience* that *he* through these words *always reveals himself anew* to those who seek him there. Thus it is certain for the believer that the words claim authority and demand obedience. God's "speaking" always demands man's "answer."

When we look at what was previously intimated concerning inspired experiences in the Old Testament and even more clearly when we study the prophets, we see what the Old Testament and the Bible as a whole mean by inspiration.[1] It is not some sort of literal "dictation" of a purely supernatural nature, as if God "bodily" appeared and audibly dictated to the prophets. Neither is it some kind of unconscious state wherein words come to the mouth and letters to the hand, as in the

[1] Cf. Sigmund Mowinckel, "'The Spirit' and the 'Word' in the Pre-exilic Reforming Prophets," *Journal of Biblical Literature,* Vol. LIII, No. 3, October, 1934, pp. 199-227.

automatic speech and writing of a medium in trance, hypnotized or self-hypnotized. The Old Testament often uses the term "Yahweh said to me" or to "so-and-so," but upon closer study we shall see that it is a shortened terminology that generally does not refer to direct speech, "mouth to mouth" or "face to face." Only in the case of Moses does the Old Testament intimate any such thing (Deut. 34:10; Num. 12:6 ff.), and even then the real meaning is problematic. Concerning the other prophets and inspired men, it is expressly said that this was not the case. It is true that "visionary" and "ecstatic" experiences with "visions" and "voices" take place among the prophets, but they themselves know very well that what they are talking about are not external but internal phenomena. The normal occurrence of inspiration within the prophets—and what they mean when they say, "The word of Yahweh came to me"—is rather an attitude of submissive and expectant inward concentration and listening, in which ideas from God arise in their minds and images form in their imagination, their inward eye, and become words to which they themselves then more or less consciously give the clearest and most impressive form possible, most frequently a rhythmic-poetic one. They ascribe no dogmatic significance to the exact wording. We see, on the contrary, that it is often formed according to poetical considerations such as rhythm and meter and pointed, powerful imagery. They themselves draw reflective conclusions from the "word" that has "come to them." They work it over in their minds and often speak in their own name. They know, however, that what they say has divine authority because it is simply the consequence of their religious-ethical "knowledge of God" acquired through their experiences and of the words that have come to them during their expectant listening. The authority of their words does not rest upon the specific wording, nor upon the "infallibility" of the form or of any detail, but upon the fact that the ideas are given to them by God for just *that* moment and just *that* situation in which they find themselves. They never stress "infallibility." On the contrary, they often had the experience that their predictions did not come about as they had expected and foretold them. This meant to them a testing, a call to self-searching (cf. Jer. 17:15), but it did not make them uncertain in their assurance that they were God's messengers and that even those words had been words of God, whatever the reason might be that they had not "come to pass" in the way that they themselves had expected. They know that they have "Yahweh's word" or "Yahweh's spirit" (Jer. 5:13; 15:16; 20:9; Isa. 61:1 ff.), and the proof that this is so is not the infallibility of the words or their outward form, but their real and essential conformity with that religious-ethical ideal and that view of God and his will that had become their spiritual possession through personal submission and personal experience of God. It had become one with their conscience, their innermost personality.

This is the core and the reality of the biblical "doctrine" of inspiration. And the disciples of the prophets, who down through the generations compiled and edited their masters' books, also had more or less of this same consciousness of calling, again more or less muddied by their own human egos.

The Principle of Solution Is a Historical View of the Bible

12. All these prophets stand with both feet in the midst of a *concrete historical situation,* speaking to their contemporaries out of it and the tasks that it imposes. For Isaiah the onward march of the Assyrians toward the Mediterranean is the background and the cause of his prophetic career. For Hosea it was the political, social, and moral dissolution of the Israelitic nation during the years before the last breakdown. For Zephaniah it was the plundering march of the Scythians. For Jeremiah both this and the tremendous encounter between Babylon and Egypt after the fall of Assyria, and so on. All this is in complete harmony with the picture that the Old Testament draws for us; that is, it is a varied and manifold history.

It always pays to look reality in the eye fairly and squarely. When we want to arrive at a comprehensive religious view of the Old Testament as God's revelation, it is this reality, that is, the historical and factual nature of the Old Testament, that we must face and make the basis of our theories. The theories have to be built upon reality, not vice versa. It may be that just such a *conclusive historical view* will *solve* the problem of the Old Testament.

Then we also should be realistic in a Christian sense and begin by asking: *What is the relationship to history in which the Old Testament and the Bible place themselves?* How does the Bible *think* about history, and how is that which takes place in the Bible *related* to history?

13. First it should be pointed out that Christ and the apostles themselves made a distinction between the revelation in the Old Testament and that which they represent, which took form in the New Testament.

The *attitude* of *Jesus to the Old Testament* is characterized by the mighty platform in the Sermon on the Mount. "You have heard that it was said . . . . But I say to you . . . ." (Matt. 5:21 ff.) Here we have words from the Old Testament discarded or transformed. In passing, we also should note that even if for Jesus the word of the Old Testament is word of God and holds divine authority, as we heard above, it does not mean that it is eternal and unchangeable. It may often represent a temporary, incomplete step in the history of revelation. It is therefore not "inerrant" in an absolute sense. Jesus knows about a commandment made "for your hardness of heart," but which really goes against God's order of creation (the law of divorce). An inner, religious-moral "critique" of the Old Testament, that is, a "distinguishing" between varied values of truth in it from the standpoint of Christianity, thus has the authority of Jesus on its side.

The basic idea with *Paul* concerning the Old Testament is that "the Law," the ritual and cultic law, which to the Jews was the cornerstone of divine revelation, has no validity for the ones "who are in Christ Jesus." Read the letters to the Romans and Galatians!

Even Jesus spoke before his death about the "New Covenant" that he came to mediate and that should replace the old one as we know it in the Old Testament. The Church has drawn the consequence of this by giving the two parts of the Bible the names: the Old and the New Covenant, the Old and the New Testament.

The sum of the biblical idea of the Old Testament in its relationship to the New Testament is that the Old Testament represents the temporary, preparatory, incomplete standpoint that has found its "fulfillment," that is, its completion and perfection, in the New Testament. It is true, Jesus said concerning his principal relationship to the Old Testament, that he did not come to "abolish" but to fulfill. "Till heaven and earth pass away, not an iota, not a dot, will pass from the law, until all is accomplished." (Matt. 5:17 ff.) But by this he did not mean that he had come to be a slave under the law nor to teach others to be so. His whole life and behavior show otherwise. He means that his goal is to "fulfill" the law, to give it a new and higher content of revelation. And insofar as the law in its very incompleteness in every point makes clear the need of something more perfect, Jesus can use the same expression otherwise used for prophecies that are fulfilled: "Not a dot, will pass from the law until all is accomplished." That which is forecast and imperfectly expressed by longings, laws, and flashes of insight is "accomplished," fulfilled, completed, when replaced by the perfection (that is, Jesus Christ himself) toward which it all pointed. "The Holy Spirit has made you guardians to feed the church of the Lord," Paul says with the same idea in mind. Christ is the goal of the Old Testament.

14. By this we mean that there exists an *organic historical relationship* between the Old Testament and the New. That is, this is a way in which we in modern terms can express the relationship. This is valid from several viewpoints.

From a *scientific view* of Christianity as a historical entity, this is self-evident. No historian would even try to describe Jesus, his teaching and work, or the apostles, early Christianity and the rise of the New Testament, without giving as a background for this a picture of Judaism and its previous development. This picture has to be taken from a historical analysis of the Old Testament. Also scientific *theology* knows that it is impossible to make such terms as "justification," "salvation," "holiness," and so on, understood without going back to their Old Testament roots and presuppositions, and beginning the description with them.

In this case, however, that which is valid for a scientific study is also valid in a *religious, a revelational* sense when seen from a "metaphysical" standpoint. The organic historical relationship between the Old Testament and the New Testament is expressed, not only in the fact that Jesus, the apostles, and early Christianity criticized the Old Testament and stressed its incompleteness and temporariness, but also, as we have just seen, that they accepted it and *built further upon it.* Because of this there are many important features of the content of Christian faith and life that are simply missing in the New Testament. The reason for this is that—when looked at from the standpoint of psychological history—these ideas were already self-evident parts of the religious consciousness of Jesus and the apostles. If we look at it from the standpoint of the religious history of revelation, it is because they were revealed earlier in the Old Testament and did not need any new revelation. The ideas lay clearly enclosed in the special experience of God as it is described in the New Testament and its content of revelation. This is especially valid for important aspects of Christian ethics, particularly for social ethics, as the relationship of the Christian to society at large: nationality, the state, and the world. The apostles simply did not need to direct their minds toward getting inspired guidance in these matters because they had them as clear principles in the Old Testament fully and concretely expressed for their needs and kept alive in the Jewish ethical heritage related to it.

15. Inside the Old Testament itself we also find clear evidences of this *double organic relationship:* a history that proceeds through *conscious break* and *conscious connection.* Through the whole Old Testament we find the consciousness of connection: the idea of *election, covenant,* a fundamental *revelation of God* at Sinai, the *kingship of Yahweh.*

On the other side, however, the Old Testament often consciously breaks with its own past. For example, it is useless to deny that the popular stories about Jacob tell about his cleverness with glee and sympathy, yet see no problem in the fact that he also was God's favorite. Insight into the unity between religion and ethics had not developed any further than this at that time, as it still has not for many Christian businessmen. The prophet Hosea, however, condemns the attitude of the patriarch in the strongest terms and finds the explanation of the corruptness and faithlessness of Israel precisely in the fact that they are descendants of the crooked and crafty Jacob; because the people are as their forefather, the judgment of death upon them is just and inescapable (12:3-4).[1] Likewise Jeremiah (9:4—9:3 in Hebrew).

At the time of Jehu the zealots for Yahweh among the prophets, both Elisha with his disciples and Jonadab ben Rechab, eagerly took part in the bloody and treacherous extinction of both the Baal worshipers and the royal house that had tolerated them; one hundred years later Hosea looks upon the bloody deed at Jezreel as one of the main reasons why Yahweh must extinguish his own people (1:4 ff.).

The many holy places around the country were long accepted as wholly legitimate; it was said that they all had their origin in a revelation of Yahweh in that place (cf. the stories of the patriarchs). In reality most of them were taken over from the Canaanites; and as time passed, they became the centers for everything in the worship of Yahweh that kept it on the same plane with the pagan religions and hindered the development of the higher religious and moral tendencies latent in Yahweh-worship. This is the reason why the prophets rejected all cultus per se: it was valueless and worse than valueless; Yahweh was in no need of cultus. It was a compromise between the prophets and the cultic religion when later it was declared permissible to worship Yahweh with sacrifices and cultic acts —but at one place only. Thereby, however, something is canceled throughout the ancient sacred history. This is especially clear in the books of Kings: the whole of ancient cultic practice is either condemned as sin or passed over in silence. All this means that men of religion are breaking with their own past and condemning it. And this in spite of the fact that in the

[1] There is a clear pun in the Hebrew *kal-ach ʿaqob ja ʿqob,* and the best rendering of the meaning is: "Every brother is a swindler (R.S.V.: a supplanter), a Jacob."

olden days they undoubtedly had both commandments and sacred traditions that explicitly demanded the whole of the old cultic worship of God; without the least doubt it was traced all the way back to Moses. Compare the situation at Dan, where the priesthood worshiped Yahweh in the form of a bull and at the same time thought of themselves as the direct descendants of Moses. (Judg. 18; cf. I Kings 12:29.)

These few examples will have to suffice. They show that both in the relationship between the Old Testament and the New and in the relationship among various streams within the Old Testament itself, we see a history unfolding, a continuity and a series of breaks: changes, growth, the discarding of the old and the creating of new forms. It is life in motion—God's life of creation and development.

In other words: The *religion of Israel* is, like Christianity, a *historical religion,* not only in the sense that it goes back to a historical person, a "founder," as we say, or at least to a certain concrete historical situation, a time of foundation, but also in the sense that it has developed and become what it is through a changing history.

And it is conscious of this! While other religions claim that their "revelations" go back to prehistoric times, to mythical antecedents and "heroes of their culture," the religion of Israel, like Christianity, understands that its revelation took place through concrete, named historical persons at various times and in connection with real concrete history. Famine forces their ancestor to Egypt. A "new king in Egypt" is the cause of Israel's departure and for their renewal of the covenant with Yahweh at Sinai, a covenant that gives the people a new revelation and religion that determine their lives for all the future. Yahweh reveals his power and guidance in the battles with the indigenous peoples. In its relations with the latter and in the correlation between the religious-ethical decay and the ups and downs of their history, Israel learns that its God is "different" from the gods of Canaan. In the politics of the great empires of the world the prophets see the drama that is to further the plan of God for his people. In the fall of Israel and Judah they see the triumph of God and the revelation of his righteousness. Let it be granted that all this is thought and told with legendary adornment (we shall later come back to this); still Israel and the Old Testament are using this form to express historical facts and the fact that Israel is bound to historical facts.

History of Revelation and History of Salvation

16. We have now arrived at the question as to *what the revelation of God is and how it takes place* in the Old Testament and the whole Bible.

The answer may be summed up as follows: Granted that ancient Israel thought, as did the surrounding religions, that the cultus in the sacred spot with the "sacraments" was the place where God was present and active, and where he made himself known through works and visions; nevertheless more and more the conscious idea emerges *that history is the real workshop of God*. There he does his works; there faith can see him and sense his secrets.[1]

The revelation of God is a *history of revelation*. This is the main view of the Old Testament. It is significant that the Old Testament ties its ideas concerning the origin of the sacred places and the sacred acts to historical persons, or at least to

[1] Cf. H. H. Rowley, *The Re-discovery of the Old Testament* (Philadelphia: The Westminster Press, 1946), pp. 83 ff. Montgomery, *op. cit.*, pp. 13 ff. Alan Richardson, *Preface to Bible-Study* (Philadelphia: The Westminster Press, 1944), pp. 42 ff.

persons whom ancient Israel held to be historical. By this they mean: It is in the real, daily world that God shows himself and is active, not in the misty world of myth and prehistoric time.

Before the prophetic movement had become the strongest spiritual power in Israel, the leading circles already had acknowledged that it was in the occurrences of history, beginning with the deliverance from Egypt, the victories over the local inhabitants, and the settlement in Canaan, that God was active and manifest (see above). In the victory over Sisera the contemporary author of the song of Deborah (Judg. 5) could see the new work of Yahweh's revelation. With the great prophets of judgment and reform this more and more becomes a leading thought. It is the occurrences of contemporary history and politics, the appearance of the Arameans, Assyrians, Babylonians, Scythians, and Persians upon the historical arena that are primarily God's word to his people (Isa. 9:7 ff.). All of history is the miracle of God. The very acts that we consider "natural" are wondrous deeds of God. The prophets made no distinction between certain happenings that were "natural" and "according to law" and others that appeared more fantastic and therefore must be God's interference with history. All is God's interference, and all has its natural side. Hence the prophets are realistic; when they are describing that which is to come, that wholly "alien" work of God (Isa. 28:21) which is to turn the world upside down, they hardly ever use that which is fantastic and of a fairy-tale nature, such as "signs in sun and moon," comets, or hosts of angels. On the contrary, they speak of the revolutionary deed that God will do through the Assyrians, through Nebuchadnezzar, through Cyrus. It is history that is the miracle, the miracle that reveals Yahweh—at the same time that which is his work and that which "unveils," "reveals" his essence, plan, and will. The nations are his tools of revelation, whether they know it or not.

In the *cultus of the feasts* ancient Israel experiences not only the presence of God and his coming, his re-creation of nature and life, but also a real repetition of his mighty work in history, of the deliverance from Egypt and the wonder at the Reed Sea (or the Red Sea).[2]

Here it is explicitly said that, just because God does these mighty works, he is "revealed." [3] The three great annual feasts in Israel were originally connected with the cycles of nature, with fertility and agricultural life. Without doubt these go back to the older Canaanite festivals, taken over and adapted by the immigrants. That which became characteristic of Israel's view of these feasts, however, was that they were a re-experiencing of the past, of history. In the cultus of the feast the wonderful history of Yahweh's revelation was created anew. Therefore, the experience of the presence of God in worship was to Israel likewise an experience of a new creation: nature was created anew, and victory was created for Israel over all her enemies. This is what the festival psalms sing about in bluntly narrative form.[4]

It is in this way that history comes alive. Nothing that happens in the world of reality is an accident. God intends something with it.

Eschatology, the ideas concerning the "last things," is also an expression of the same belief: that God has a purpose, that

[2] See especially the so-called "Enthronement Psalms," Pss. 47, 93, 95–100, and autumn and new year festival psalms such as 46, 65, 75, 76, 81, and others. See to this S. Mowinckel, *Psalmenstudien II* (Videnskapsselsk. Skr. II Hist. Filos. Kl., Kr.a., 1921, No. 6).

[3] Pss. 9:17; 48:4; 76:2; 77:15; Isa. 40:5; 53:1.

[4] Pss. 46, 47, 48, 65, 75, 76, 81, 85, 95–100, and 149.

he has a plan to be realized, a goal to be reached, and that all the occurrences in history point toward this. Even if the goal is realized through a divine miracle, the historic realities are the means of this miracle. In harmony with this view faith for the Old Testament is the ability to see the creative work of God in history. This is especially evident with Isaiah.[5] For this very reason the prophets also demand that practical politics should be carried out according to divine guidance (Isa. 7–8, 30).

It is in connection with this faith in a living revelation that belief in the one God emerged. It begins with Yahweh's determining that which takes place in the history of *Israel* and in her clashes with the neighboring peoples. In the end Yahweh is guiding *all* history and doing all things: he becomes the one true God, the only one to deserve that name.

It is significant that the first two literary works of any size in Israel, the "Yahwist" and the "Elohist," which are the oldest main sources for the Pentateuch and the other historical books, tell about God in the form of history; their intention is to unveil his nature and his ways through the saga. To understand the plan of God is, for them, to understand history as God's history.[6] Yahweh, the God of history—this is the thought that more than anything else distinguishes the religion of Israel from the neighboring religions.

As far as *Christianity* is concerned, not many words are needed to show that its concept of revelation is oriented to history. It accepted the whole history of the Old Testament as revelation, and from the beginning it has seen the perfect revelation

[5] S. Mowinckel, *Profeten Jesaja* (Oslo: H. Aschehoug & Co., 1925), pp. 88-94.

[6] A. Weiser, *Die theologische Aufgabe der alttestamentlichen Wissenschaft* (Stuttgart: W. Kohlhammer, 1936), p. 7.

of God in the historical man Jesus Christ and in that which happened to him and through him. Therefore: *Revelation takes place as a history of revelation.*

17. This idea of God as the God of history, and of history as the place of revelation, also clearly shows what the Bible means by revelation. It is not communication of knowledge, theoretical truths from and about God. Yes, it is too, but only secondarily and derivatively. Primarily and essentially *revelation is deed;* it is God's work of creating anew and of creating the future that is his revelation. All the places alluded to above show this clearly: it is through his miraculous work that God is "revealed," is "acknowledged," "makes himself known," "unveils himself." Through *his word* he "unveils himself" (cf. Isa. 22:14) just as much as the word prophesies about and interprets his work, for the word itself *is* to the Israelite a deed, a *miracle* (Isa. 9:8). The word *of God,* and thereby also the inspired word of the prophet, is "dynamically acting power; it is in itself a factor in history." When the "word" "light[s] upon Israel," it works like a destructive explosion (Isa. 9:8). Hosea can let God say, "I have slain them by the words of my mouth" (6:5). Jeremiah knows himself sent "to destroy and . . . to build" (1:10), and the word of God in his mouth becomes a fire that will consume the people like wood (5:14). And to the extent that the revelation is communication of knowledge —common truths about God and his being and work and plan, and about the world and man in his relationship to God —to that extent "seeing faith" cannot help drawing such conclusions from its vision of the God who works this way in the real world.

This does not mean that the revelation of God in history is

only partial and indirect. On the contrary: it is God's work in history that is his most authentic and direct revelation. Because there he himself is present, not just philosophical truths about him.

In this way revelation in reality becomes an unfolding of the creative work of God. *Creation* and *revelation* are correlative terms, or rather: realities. Creation in the Bible is not a once terminated act. For the old Israel, God's coming in the cultus of the festival was a repetition and a continuance of creation just as it also repeated history; "My Father is working still," Jesus says. As God unveiled himself and his plan in Creation, so he continues to reveal himself in history. Paul expresses the same truth in more philosophical terms when he is speaking of the revelation of God that each man has or at least could have from the work of creation—herein is included the moral consciousness of man—and that would have been sufficient if man only had been willing to open himself to it and follow it (Rom. 1:19 ff. 2:14 ff.).

18. All this also implies that the *history of revelation in reality is also history of salvation.* The plan of God is ultimately his plan of salvation; the intent of creation is salvation, the full realization of God's goal; "all things were created through him and for him" (Col. 1:16). For salvation in its full biblical meaning is not only salvation *from,* but also salvation *to* something. It is the realization of the kingdom of God. It is our sin that causes it also to be a salvation *from* something. All the work of God, therefore, even when he judges and punishes, in reality is part of his plan and work of salvation. The history of salvation is that which God actually has done and is doing for our salvation and the world's. It is precisely in this work and by this goal that he "reveals" himself, shows who and what he is and what he wills.

To say, therefore, that God reveals himself really means, according to the Bible, that he *gives himself*. Not knowledge about himself, but himself. He gives himself in and by his creative and saving (re-creative) work.

The proof for this is *Christ*. In Christ, God gave himself to the world and for the salvation of the world. In Christ he identified himself with us, with all our sin, shame, misery, and mortality; gave himself fully; made himself "flesh," yea, even "sinful flesh," as Paul expresses it. Christ is God in his self-sacrificing, self-revealing, and saving love. He is the perfect revelation of God.

The Biblical Ideas About Word of God

19. As we take a look at what the Bible means by *"word of God,"* we can see that this is correct. Here also the Old Testament ideas find their full content in the New Testament.

As has been mentioned already, for the Old Testament, God's word is not utterances, not verbal expressions of ideas, concepts, and thoughts, but *deed.* It expresses an activity, a personal will to effect that which lies in the being of God. It creates what it names. When God "sent a word against Jacob," then this means in the given situation a desolating change, a bomb that explodes (Isa. 9:8 ff.). It never returns empty but effects that which it is sent to do (Isa. 55:10 ff.). It expresses the being of God; it *is,* so to speak, the being of God in outgoing activity. When it "comes to"—or more correctly "becomes active reality in"—the prophets, then it is a power that fills them, revolutionizes their personal lives, and has to be transformed into action: as, for instance, into the devastating "wrath of Yahweh" against the unfaithful people (Jer. 6:11; 20:9); or it is "a hammer which breaks the rock in pieces" (Jer. 23:29) and that often recasts the fate of the peoples and the lands. It is the very power of God that created the world and constantly creates anew (Gen. 1; Ps. 33:9; 107:20); it is also the power that creates religious and moral life in the individual and the people (Pss. 19, 119). And significantly, the conception usually is not that the written or formulated work is there first and then causes this effect; rather it is God's own creative intervention that *is* the "word" and that *also* transforms itself into concepts, ideas, thoughts, and visions in those to whom "it comes." It is understandable that the word sometimes in the Old Testament appears as an independent "person" beside God (a "hypostasis"—see Pss. 33:6; 107:20; 147:15; Isa. 55:11) and as one having divine characteristics (cf. Isa. 40:8; Ps. 33:4)—wherever this happens, what is implied by "the Word" is the *whole essence* of *God.*

The same features are found again in the ideas of the New Testament about Word of God.[1] This is especially so in the ideas found in the Gospel of John about the "Word," *Logos,* that yield a lively picture. Logos here means not only the spoken Word of God, but also the thought of God, his intent, God's intelligent plan for the world, as the motive power and the expression of his activity that it has been from eternity. It is the transmitter of all the divine characteristics, of God's essence and power. It mediated the creation of the world and constantly creates life anew. It gives light in darkness; it mediates religious and moral awakening, conversion, re-creation, life, and insight. It has within itself the whole fullness of the Godhead and yet stands as if it were independently side by side with God. It is God in his self-revealing, judging and saving activity. But that which the New Testament most clear-

[1] Cf. John 8:27; 12:48; Col. 3:16; II Thess. 3:1; II Tim. 2:9; Tit. 2:5; I Pet. 1:23; Heb. 4:12-13.

ly adds to the Old Testament is the knowledge that this Word of God *"became flesh."* God gave himself to us and for us in the fact that the Word, which had been at work since before the creation of the world, became flesh in the historical man Jesus Christ. It is through this incarnation that God entered history in all his fullness of power and essence; it is through it that the perfect revelation of God took place. God in his character of active Word became historical man and identified himself with us and our sins. Thereby he has lifted us out of them and adopted us to sonship with himself. It is revelation, self-communication, and salvation all at once, realized in history as divine deed.

20. Compared with these concrete ideas about the Word, the concept of the *Spirit of God* as a medium of revelation is less stressed in the Bible. Aside from the fact that the older passages in the Old Testament preferably connect "the Spirit of Yahweh" with ecstatic experiences, the real content of the idea is largely the same as in the idea of "the Word of Yahweh." The Spirit also is an expression of the revealing activity of God, and it is seen first of all as creative power, working in history through the men who are leaders in history. This is made especially clear in the stories about the "Judges" and the first kings. The Spirit works as inspiration, as divine power creating thought, words, and deeds, not only in the prophets and the apostles, but also in all true believers, in whom it creates new religious and moral life. It is in this way that the Spirit is the revealer of God and Christ in the world.

Speaking of revelation in a narrow sense, in thought and word, there is in the Old Testament no essential distinction between the expression "the Word of God came to" and "the

Spirit of God came upon," or "said to." Even the mental process involved is conceived in the same way, except, as mentioned, for the more ecstatic factor that in older times was connected with the concept of the Spirit of God.

21. To sum up what has been said in these two sections (19 and 20) : the view that originates in the Bible itself is that the revelation of God "is not knowledge of some fact which somehow and somewhere exists and is perceived by thought, but knowledge of a reality which occurs and is perceived by acting and suffering with that which occurs." [2] The revelation of God is God's own self-giving activity and the religious-moral life and the religious-moral insight that is created by it. It unfolds itself through history in the widest sense of this term: that which actually occurs. History in both the cosmic and the earthly sense is the great drama played for the salvation of the world; it is in this drama that God "makes himself known."

[2] Weiser, *op. cit.*

A Religio-Historical Study of the Old Testament—A Necessary Theological Task

22. If revelation is God's self-giving activity in history, then it is also an important *theological task,* and not just one of profane history, to obtain the clearest possible *picture of the real history* that lies behind the testimony of the Old Testament, so far as this is possible with the limited means of human science and insight. What we must try to reach, as far as we can grasp it, is not an idealized history, which tinkers with the sources and the facts according to our Christian wishes and ideals, but the naked facts. And this we must do even though our recognition of the facts often includes an admission that we do not know very much about certain matters, even though the sources, sometimes at first glance, may seem to give considerable data about them (as, for instance, in the case of Israel's entrance into Egypt and its exodus, the covenant at Sinai, and much else). We are thus speaking of a historical theology aided by historical and philological criticism.

This task, which in the first instance is strictly scientific, also has a practical significance. For, of course, "accurate observation" and "honest exegesis" should also be the basic rule for a practical, edifying use of the Bible. This includes the duty to obtain the clearest possible picture of "when, where, who, to whom, how, under what circumstances," that is, all that concretizing and visualizing of the situation under study that can be obtained only through historical study and investigation. In order to translate this into a corresponding message relevant to our situation, we have the further duty of finding out as exactly as possible what the point in the passage is, what God wanted to give to specific people in *their* specific situation. This concrete light upon the details in history, however, can be gained only from a clear and well-founded total view of the spiritual history of Israel. As this in turn is built up out of details, there is a constant interplay with many possibilities of error and ever-new problems—as in all science.

23. It is also clear, however, that Christianity and theology cannot be content with a purely secular historical view, with a critical registration of more or less certain (or uncertain) facts and their more or less clear inner and outer relationships of cause and effect in geography, economics, ideology, and so on. What is important for theology is to arrive at a *supramundane meaning in history,* its goal, what God intended and did with history.

The direction in which we are moving is indicated by what has been said: namely, that Christ is the center of revelation and of the history of salvation; he is the axis around which history turns.

It may be of some interest to point out that the task itself, the urge toward such an evaluating scrutiny of history, a "philosophy of history," is not a theological invention violating scholarship. *Profane historical inquiry* has also constantly tended toward such a view. For history means movement from something to something. A movement, naturally, *can* be completely "accidental," that is, without rule or goal. If this is so, then any hope for scientific understanding is out of the question. Scientific understanding stands and falls with the "law of causality," which may be no law for reality itself, but at least is a law for our thinking and perception of reality. It develops within us by our noticing a certain regularity and constancy in that which takes place. Therefore all practical life and all theoretical thinking reckon with it. Consequently the idea of a certain direction in the movement of history is suggested, a direction instead of absolutely blind chance.

It is evident, however, that it is not thereby proved that the movement of history really has a goal. Even a direction may be an eternal movement without a goal; it might, for instance, run back upon itself and create an eternal circle. But the urge to find a goal is there, and all serious consideration of coherence in history has led to the idea of a goal. Thus it is very significant that the view of history that calls itself "materialistic" and that in theory tries to be strictly mechanistic energetically posits a goal: economic "development" suddenly becomes a mystical, metaphysical-divine principle with a will and a goal, which necessarily leads man through a series of crises toward the ideal society of socialism. (After which movement ceases? Or what *does* happen?)

In reality, however, no mechanistic-materialistic or psychological-ideological view of history, nor any view that is simply immanent, considering only "intramundane" factors, can lead to a positive answer about the goal and meaning of history.

Science can give only causal connection, necessity, determinism —and unveil the need for something more!

Christian faith also knows about necessity, about the bound will (*servum arbitrium*). It even knows that the will is bound to evil (*perversa voluntas*). It also, however, knows the concept of "guilt," and guilt means that I *know* that I both should and could have chosen otherwise than I did. Christian faith knows also that "over," or "behind"—or "under"—my "necessities," and "causal connection," my "determination by inheritance" and my "determination by environment," stands another power that is both I and not-I, and that lays upon me the responsibility for my choice, sets a goal for my decisions, and leads me toward it. Faith knows also that this is valid, not only for me, but for man as such, indeed for the whole universe.

Christian faith, alone, can *give meaning to history,* and it insists upon doing so. The goal and meaning are given by the term "the kingdom of God"; and the gate to this kingdom is Christ, and history's course is the way to Christ.

This means that faith acknowledges scientific ideas concerning causal relationships and "natural" powers in history. It means that it must acknowledge development, "evolution." This word in Christian circles has often been felt to be the very opposite of a history of revelation and salvation directed by God. But this is incorrect. The word itself does not indicate that what takes place is through immanent powers; the word merely signifies continuous direction toward a goal. If it is true that history is movement, direction, and destination toward a goal, something dynamic and not static, then it presupposes evolution.

In fact, it is impossible to conceive of an orderly coherence in that which takes place without using the idea of evolution.

All scientific thinking, and also all the practical uses of science, for instance, in biology and racial hygiene, agriculture and cattle breeding, take it into account and act accordingly.

The idea of evolution, however, gives no one any right to abolish or reject the idea of free choice and to assert a blind mechanical necessity. Neither does it abolish moral evaluation. In human life, in spiritual life, both good and evil are real powers; evolution does not abolish the fact of dualism. At every single moment, in every single situation, the tension of dualism is there. For Christian faith this is an unrelinquishable reality.

Evolution means organic coherence, linear movement, in that which takes place. The idea of evolution, therefore, finds full positive content only through the idea of teleology—in the idea that the line points toward a goal.

Such an idea is not at all contradictory to Christian faith in God; on the contrary, it is demanded by faith in God.

That which faith must demand is that the goal and direction be willed, wrought, and guided by *God,* that the "coherences" and "natural" relationships be the means by which God effects his goal, even though in most instances it is impossible to indicate exactly how they fit into the plan of divine guidance or what God's plan is with just *these* things.

24. On the other hand, it is not satisfactory for Christian faith to think of the course of the world and history as a machine that is started and runs all by itself, with which God once in a while "interferes" by a "miracle." This would mean making creation too independent of the Creator; it would mean co-ordinating the two as factors of the same nature. Christian faith does not say "God and medicine"; it knows that it is normally "God *through* medicine." In spite of this, however, faith also must use the term "interfere." This, too, mythically expresses God's sovereign relationship to his work. It also expresses something else: namely, that my sin cannot destroy God's goal or frustrate his achievement of it. Even if my sin crosses and hinders his plan, he is, figuratively speaking, man enough to "relink the chain of events," to make the situation created by my sin into a new starting point, to give it a positive meaning. This is what we mean when we say that "God interfered in my life."

For Christian faith, history is at the very same time something "natural," a continuous organic stream of life that unfolds itself and that we can see from the angle of cause and effect, *and* in addition something willed and guided by God, that is, history with a goal.

It is in the latter that theology has to find the line of motion. This is its task of discovering a history of revelation and of salvation.

Everything stands in a "natural" continuity, and science has to try to explain this while aware of the fact that with its own means it can never completely explain it. And *everything* is a link in the plan of God; even sin and evil he can "link in" to his plan and give them meaning.

The Old Testament as a Link in God's Special Revelation

25. But then one will ask: If history as a whole is the place of God's revelation, how can one say that the Old Testament is word of God more than other books of religion from the period prior to Christ? What is the difference between the history of the Old Testament and all other history?

26. In order to answer this, we first must look at another important side of history. It is that which Hempel calls its *Einmaligkeit,* its "once-for-all-ness." It cannot be repeated or revoked. *Wer Geschichte sagt, sagt Einmaligkeit.* History never repeats itself. Thereby it apparently distinguishes itself from natural occurrences, which to our eyes are seen to repeat themselves with regularity: "While the earth remains, seedtime and harvest, cold and heat, summer and winter, day and night, shall not cease" (Gen. 8:22). In history there has been but one Guatama Buddha, one Mohammed, both of whom have irrevocably changed the fate of a great part of mankind, spiritually and materially. There has been but one battle at Stiklestad with decisive effect upon all the history of Norway and one battle of the Marne, which determined the result of the First World War.

This irrevocability of history is connected with the free will of man. We cannot here note the problem of determinism—indeterminism. It cannot be solved logically and philosophically. Life itself, however, must be lived as if both prevailed; it must be lived dialectically. In spite of the fact that we are inescapably bound to think in terms of causality, we never can get around the fact that life consists of a continuous series of choices and decisions, in which I *know* that I can answer either "yes" or "no." Even if my answer often has the character of an "I must," "I can do no other," this "must" often is an inner "must," which has its root in the fact that I have placed myself under a "something," a value that is greater than I and to which I submit just because I acknowledge it to be superior to me in value. I know also that in this very subordination my liberty consists. I am not free until I have cast off my connection with the lesser value and said an unconditional "yes" to the higher one. I also know that if I say "no" when my inner obligation demands that I say "yes," then I am *guilty* in so doing. If I see deeply enough into myself, I see also in my "no" a depraved determinism of the will, an evil fatalism: I cannot even will that which is good (witness Rom. 7!). But I know also that within me there is "another law" that judges this as guilt and says: You very well know that it could have been otherwise!

Unfolding history is exactly the actualization of these decisions of the human will. Even from the standpoint of science it is shortsighted to deny that a decision of a single individual is an important factor in creating history in spite of all the "forces" and "laws" whether economic or otherwise. It is upon this co-operation of many factors that the irrevocability of history, its "once-for-all-ness," depends.

True, one can also speak about *historical "laws,"* and a comparative study of culture tries to find common laws for that which takes place in the world of language, religion, art, society, and economics. It is also correct to say that the limits that reality itself sets upon the range of variety in our choices indicate that also in other human lives similar decisions with similar results are constantly being made in similar situations. Each of these links, however, has its own special individualization. The "laws" that one can thus discover are nothing but relatively loose-fitting types of phenomena. Under no circumstances do they have the character of anything else but laws of a statistical average, an abstract scheme for the more or less varied concrete cases and individual phenomena.

27. From this "once-ness" of history light falls upon the Old Testament as the *revelation of God in a more special sense* than in any other ancient history: what the old dogmaticians called *revelatio specialis,* "special revelation," to be kept distinct from *revelatio generalis,* the "common revelation" in nature, intelligence, conscience, and history.

Historical "continuity" in the opinion of science encompasses all history. It is also contrary to the biblical view of God as the God of history to assume that there is history that has not been guided by him and that does not have connection with his plan. If there are a goal and a meaning in history, then there is also a certain *line* in it that shows the direction and the goal. Naturally there are many lines that may be followed in history, but for Christian faith there is only one, the main line. It is part of the once-ness of history that if we try to discover and follow a certain line, then it runs through definite points. It is through the concrete unique incidents that a certain historical line becomes apparent. If we, for example, want to follow a certain idea, for instance the idea of humaneness in history, then there are millions of known and unknown factors that have played a part. The main line, however, runs through specific persons and epochs and incidents, which then mark out the meaning of history for us from *this* standpoint.

The question then is: Where does the genuine main line of the history of salvation run, the line that through all the preparatory steps and incidents leads to true ethical monotheism, true grace and salvation, true re-creation, true participation in the Spirit of God, true universalism, the true kingdom of God —in short, the line to and through Christ?

The answer must be: It runs through the Old Testament, through Israel and Judaism, including late Judaism (the age of the Apocrypha and apocalyptics). There is only one Christ and one Calvary. The way to Calvary ran from Galilee to Jerusalem. The historical line ran from Mesopotamia through Canaan to Jerusalem, with many loops (to Egypt, for instance), but it is easy to follow. It is evident also that even a purely secular historical study must come to the same conclusion, regardless of how much it might come to discover about foreign influences upon the culture and religion of Israel.

A presentation of the development in the religious history of Israel and Judaism will make this clear; and as I have maintained above, this is a necessary theological task. It is precisely the genuine, legitimate tendencies in this religion that lead to Christianity, to Jesus and Paul and the Christian solution to the problems of the early ancient Church. Even a secular historical study will have to affirm that orthodox rabbinic Judaism is that branch of the common tree that leads away from the main tendency, which allows the development to bend backward again and end in a blind alley from which it cannot escape without a radical conversion. The assertion that rabbinism is "normative Judaism" must even from a strictly historical standpoint be reckoned as a mistake.

28. For such a sketch of Old Testament history of religion there will be no room here. I shall point only to another important relationship, which also shows that the line to the New Testament runs through the Old Testament: namely, *the structural relationship between the Old Testament and the New.*

That with which both the Old Testament and the New Testament are ultimately concerned is the righteousness of God. This means in both places much more than is commonly understood in nontheological language. We may explain the main idea like this: Righteousness is at the same time the actuating principle of the being and work of God and the demands he presents on the basis of these. It is also the principle of "salvation," the acknowledgment of and the fellowship with himself and the quality of life that he gives those who will accept it. It contains at the same time both the demand, the law—and the grace, the gospel.

In the Old Testament it is this understanding that works its way to the fore. In the older levels of the Old Testament these two main parts of "righteousness" lie interwoven in naïve unity. The "righteous man" is he who has the nature and "blessedness" in him to do, together with the divine powers that are in him, what is right and will reap the fruits of blessing. This is also true of the people as a whole. Especially is this "righteousness" present in the leaders of the tribe as those who thereby uphold it and "save" it. Most of all it is found in the Deity himself, who thereby maintains his own being and the "peace" and "salvation" of his covenant people. The holy and righteous God implants fear; but the Israelite will say, "Is not your fear . . . your confidence?" (Job 4:6). Fear is good; it is a virtue, because it is the covenant God who implants it. Fear of God expels all other fear and thereby creates trust and love. Precisely fear and weakness for the Israelite became a generator of trust. This is also true from a Christian standpoint, where its validity rests upon the atoning work of Jesus Christ. In Israel this faith was still naïve and built upon a superficial knowledge of human nature. It therefore had to be shattered. The shattering of the naïve view was prepared through the social development, and in the preaching of the prophets the two sides of God's nature stand in dialectical tension. His love (grace) is absolute and shows itself in his unconditional election and covenant with a people who in themselves did not deserve it. To this corresponds his demand of unconditional surrender, faithfulness, and obedience. But because the people did not follow this demand at a single point, but in a sinful sense of security rested upon the election, sin became absolute—that is, total—depravity. This raises a problem in the preaching of the prophets, in which the prophets of doom assert that the absolute love that demands everything turns into absolute hatred (cf. Jer. 12:8). In contrast to this, Deutero-Isaiah and the restoration prophets after him argue that God's absolute love prevails within him, and therefore he will himself re-create the people so that it may be able to fulfill his demands. This reminds us of the famous prayer of Augustine: "Give what Thou demandest, then demand whatever Thou wilt."

But how is this to be achieved? The Old Testament does not give any answer to this problem; what happens is that the whole thing is pushed out into the future as a dream. The New Testament gives the answer: that it takes place through God's giving himself in Christ and identifying himself with us, reconciling us to himself. This answer not only is theoretical in the sense that this is the way in which it has to be thought of or this is the way it will happen at some time in the eschatological future; but the New Testament says that *now* is the eschatological moment, the "acceptable" time (II Cor. 6:2). From now on the kingdom of heaven is taken by force by those who have the power of God in themselves (Matt. 11:12). The answer of the New Testament is reality; the gospel is just this: that God has acted decisively, and Christ is a reality! In the Cross of Christ the unity of God's holy righteousness and love are made real, and in such a way that it at the same time judges and restores. It frees and restores *through* crushing and condemning. Therefore, the content of the revelation of salvation that is preached in the New Testament is: sin is total depravity, and God's condemnation of sin—which he in Christ has taken upon himself—is unconditional, but God exercises grace. The content of his paradoxical grace is that he justifies sinners by taking upon himself their sin and acquitting them and re-creating them. This means that the broken covenant is restored; God elects a new people of God both from those of the former people who will receive it and from the Gentiles who through the fulfillment of the history of revelation had been prepared to receive the election. With this new people he makes a new covenant.

The Old Testament history of revelation ends by pointing beyond itself to the "last things," an eschatological time when God makes all things new and dissolves the tension. Fumbling and groping, it points to the vicarious suffering of the righteous one as the way forward (cf. Yahweh's servant in Isa. 53). The New Testament begins by saying, "Today this scripture has been fulfilled in your hearing" (Luke 4:21). The ultimate wonder, the end, the last things, have become reality in the midst of us. In and through the appearance of Jesus and his work the kingdom of God is in our midst (Matt. 12:28; Luke 17:21) with the powers that will create anew the heavens and the earth and make men new.

The development and clarification of this tension between "law" and "gospel" *is* history itself, is revelation, is the preparation of salvation in the Old Testament. It *is* revelation as sacred history truly lived and experienced. Thus from this central point the individual problems of the Old Testament find their theological clarification. This must be the critical principle for the theological study of the Old Testament.

The Election of Israel

29. Precisely because history for the Christian is divinely guided history, in which all events have a peculiar value once and for all, faith and theology cannot be satisfied with a mere catalogue of the ideological connection of events made from the standpoint of secular history. For our faith must maintain that the "line" in the Old Testament means what theology has called the *special revelation* to Israel, and it must also maintain the seemingly paradoxical and sometimes obnoxious idea of the *election of Israel.* This is another demonstration of the idea of God's intervention as it must be formulated with regard to total history. It is, therefore, also significant that in every place where God's "intervention" is felt to be revolutionizing life, there the idea of "election" or "predestination" presents itself at once. This is true also in the situation of the individual. In this thought Jeremiah finds the solution to his life (1:5), and here Paul sees the innermost secret in the divine decision concerning his destiny. Thus it is through the election that the "intervention" is realized which denotes the special revelation through Israel.

This means that through a special people in a specific place and through concrete personalities and incidents that have formed their outer and inner history God has drawn his line of revelation and salvation in history, and it is clearly visible and appropriable as both religious understanding and creative reality. And this is so whether we see it from the angle of religious understanding or as an objective act of salvation. God chose this people in order to bring about this history through them, and with this in view he guided the outward and inner history of both this people and the whole Near East—and faith will affirm that of all mankind too. In Old Testament history everything has its place, even the apostasies, even sagas and legends, even foreign influences, just as my sins have their place in the history through which God has led me.

One may ask why God has chosen just *this* people. Isn't such arbitrariness an injustice? If one takes a standpoint that is either non-Christian or purely formal and logical, no one can answer. The Old Testament itself has only this one answer: that it is out of pure love and grace. This in reality is the only answer that can be given. But in the preparatory and incomplete nature of the revelation that the Old Testament had, the Old Testament still could not see the whole answer. The common view held by Israel and Judaism conceived of election as preferential and partisan love for Israel. Against this view of election and the covenant the prophets raise their protest out of actual situations in their day. A clear understanding, however, of the *universal* nature of the idea of election was reached neither by Amos, who began the criticism of the common view (Amos 3:2; 9:7), nor by Deutero-Isaiah, the most universalistic of all the prophets.[1] In "the songs of the Servant

[1] Trying to read a clearly universalistic, that is, a Christian, understanding of

of the Lord" it lies unexpressed in the background.[2] But in Christ we know what it means: namely, love toward the whole world. It was an election of one as a means to reach all.

Someone may still object: But why Israel? Why not, for example, the "Aryans?" The answer is: "Because it had to be thus," or "I do not know!" An analogy, however, may clarify the matter to some degree. If I have confidence in God, I believe that the experiences and incidents of my life that led me to Christ were exactly those which God saw could lead me there and which he, therefore, "chose." Then it means nothing whether I myself or others would have preferred that it be through other incidents, persons, or movements that I had reached Christ.

He who has faith in God as guiding history must see it the same way: that it was through just these incidents that he could reach his goal. Faith must accept the fact that God's ways are not ours—or rather: it is self-evident to faith that such is the case. Perhaps the very stumbling block, which for many the choice of Israel has once more become,[3] is also part of God's plan, part of the challenge and the call to humility that the gospel always is. Our "Aryan" pride perhaps once more has to be crushed upon the stone that is placed in Zion (Isa. 28:16; Rom. 9:33; Matt. 21:44).

However, it is important to realize clearly what the consequences of the election are. Amos saw this: "You only have I known of all the families of the earth; therefore I will punish

election out of Gen. 1–11, or out of the words of blessing to the patriarchs in Gen. 12:3; 22:18, and so on, is nonhistorical leveling, which in reality deprives Christianity of its originality.

[2] Isa. 42:1-4; 49:1-6; 50:4-11; 52:13–53:12.

[3] Remember that this was written in Europe in 1937. Hitler is being parodied with "Aryan." (Translator's note.)

you for all your iniquities" (Amos 3:2). God's election is always an election for service, humiliation, suffering. And it is said of Paul: "He is a chosen instrument of mine to carry my name before the Gentiles and kings and the sons of Israel; for I will show him how much he must suffer for the sake of my name" (Acts 9:15-16). The Old Testament begins to see that this is so in the songs of the suffering servant of the Lord. But that suffering should be the privilege of Israel, Judaism could not see. We first see this revealed in Jesus Christ, who here unveils the deepest divine secret of life, that life and the possibility of life lie in and are unveiled in a loving willingness to give oneself for others, as the cross demonstrates so clearly. The elect himself experiences it, paradoxically enough, as a love that honors him: "We rejoice in our sufferings" (Rom. 5:3). "But rejoice in so far as you share Christ's sufferings, that you may also rejoice and be glad when his glory is revealed." (I Pet. 4:13.)

Away from Relativism!

30. That the Old Testament really is God's revelation in a special sense, as we have tried to show in the preceding sections (22-29), probably is the deepest problem for the theologian since historical-scientific theology arose. Because the whole of modern historical and psychological science has created a mood that makes it natural for us to give only relative validity to all ideas and ideals, moral and religious, everything is connected with certain historical relationships, with heredity and environment; everything is conditioned by something else. Moral concepts and their origin can be followed both historically and psychologically, and one can see how they have changed down through the shifting ages. The same is true of religious, social, and political ideas and ideals. How, then, can they have any absolute validity? Is there anything absolute?

At the same time we have experienced since the First World War how crippling this relativism is for all life. It is directly hostile to life. Men are tired of relativism and are looking around for something absolute that can both secure their lives and give them content. This is most clearly seen in the political sphere, in which people cry for authority, not out of some theoretical interest or inferiority on the part of individuals, but from a general and really felt need and anxiety.

It is, therefore, important to consider this problem of relativity. Theology cannot get around it. It is most clearly raised in the Old Testament and becomes a problem about revelation itself. How can anything that has developed in history, that is, in relativity, have absolute and eternal significance? The problem is pointed up even more in Christ, for how can a historical person be at the same time the absolute center of history far above all relativity?

The real answer to this question is, of course, the total surrender of mind, will, and whole person that is called faith, and that assures one that God is God, and also thereby leads to the assurance that Christ is more than a historical person in a world of relativity, that he at the same time is the "Son of God." Nothing but this faith can enable us to see revelation and word of God in the Old Testament or in the Bible as a whole.

But honest thinking also wants to know how and why. And as the acknowledgment of "the once-for-all-ness" of history helped to explain how the Old Testament reflected God's revelation in a more special sense than other religious history does, it appears that it may also prove helpful in aiding one to get beyond relativity in the historical perspective.

It is then worth noting that this "law of nonrepeatability" is found not only in history and in the life of the human spirit, but also in the natural world. In spite of all their conditioning by fate and natural law, there are no two men completely alike. This holds for both soul and body. There are no two fingerprints in the world that are identical; neither are two leaves in the forest completely alike. The "law of individualization" is just as valid as that of "generalization." That remnant of incalculability the scientist finds when it comes to the behavior of electrons leaves natural law with only the relative validity of statistical probability. This seems also to indicate that here too the law of individualization is dominant, for no two electrons seem to be identical either.

Also in biology we meet the unique event that achieves decisive significance for "all" the future. We meet, for instance, the mutation that gives the life of a certain species a new direction, a mutation that goes back to a single individual in a definite situation. Since, for instance, there are species of fish that leave the water, this most probably goes back to one specimen of the species that for some unknown reason got this urge, or whose brood was born with it. Since man also "developed"—a term that can easily be misunderstood—from a species of animal, that was probably because at a certain point in time there suddenly existed a being that gave a new direction to the line of progression—that is, because at a certain point in time there appeared an individual whom we can correctly and justly call the first created man.

On the basis of such reflections as these it becomes easier for our minds to grasp the fact that in history—and in the wider sense the animals also belong to "history"—unique persons and unique incidents have had decisive importance for all the future. Thus entities appear that have eternal significance for us.

It is worth while here to point to the biblical parallel between the "first Adam" and the "second Adam," Christ, and to the term that Jesus used of himself: "the Son of man," that is, "man." These are ideas on a similar plane. Just as there once arose in history a first Adam, whose significance for humanity was absolute, so in the center of history there arose a "second Adam," whose significance has been absolute both for mankind and for all the creation in bondage (Rom. 8:20 ff.). There have been *one* Jesus of Nazareth and *one* Golgotha, and upon these rests the eternal fate of all mankind. They signify that God has broken vertically into history and that he has planted something absolute in this world of relativity.

The Limitation of History in Time

31. The Old Testament and the Bible as a whole do not claim to be a textbook in cosmogony or cosmology, history or physics, metaphysics or any other science. As revelation, according to its deepest divine purpose, it wants to do nothing but set men in relationship with God, give the truth of God to men. It wants to do nothing but witness and teach what will cause men, just where they are, to know themselves and their deep need for salvation and God and his never-ending urge to save, and to point the way to this salvation. "To witness to sin and grace" would be the traditional expression, or to use the expression of Luther, "to impel toward Christ." All that it says in laws, stories, exhortations, promises, threats, teaching, and prayer has only the intention to get sin and grace before the minds of men. That is why the Bible is so varied, speaking in so many ways and from so many situations, presuppositions, and levels of culture. This is done in order to confront the individual at various levels and in the different situations in which he stands.

This may be illustrated with some examples: The Bible does not tell about Creation in order to tell how the world became a reality, but in order to witness concerning God and to proclaim his power, his world plan and his glory (cf. Ps. 8).

The Old Testament *faith in creation* has to be distinguished from Old Testament *views* of creation. These views are mostly borrowed from ancient Oriental sources. This article of Old Testament faith sprang not at all from a neutral interest in knowledge about the order and origin of the world. It serves, rather, as an expression of divine activity that here and now encompasses him who confesses this faith and makes his own situation before God clear to him, whether this takes place from the standpoint of the whole people as an acknowledgment of the unity of creation, history, hope for the future as it is expressed by Deutero-Isaiah, or in individual form as in Ps. 22:10 ff., where faith in creation as faith in being "cast upon God from birth" is the last resort of the praying person in his distress, or it may be as in Ps. 139:13 ff., as a confession from a man who in wonder becomes conscious of how his whole existence is surrounded by God's miraculous power.[1]

In spite of Luke 1:4, the Gospels really do not tell of Jesus in order to instruct the historically interested about his life and "teaching," but in order to awaken faith in him as Christ, as God's perfect revelation (John 20:31).

The biblical narrators do not tell their sagas for the sake of the saga nor for the sake of historical interest, but in order to give a testimony about God, his being and plan. In reality, therefore, they write for *our* sake (Rom. 15:4).

The lawbooks of Israel did not become a part of the Bible of the Church in order to be law for the Christian, but in order to awaken the recognition of sin and the need for salvation and

[1] A. Weiser, *Die theologische Aufgabe der alttestamentlichen Wissenschaft* (Stuttgart: W. Kohlhammer, 1936), pp. 8-9.

to exhort people to find the will of God for their specific circumstances (cf. Rom. 7–8).

It makes no difference, therefore, whether the original transmitters of the material or the Old Testament authors themselves may have thought, for instance, that it was very important for one's faith and relationship to God to know how the world began, or to know what kings had ruled in Judah and Israel. When we look at the Old Testament as a whole from the standpoint of the history of revelation, it does not matter, for instance, what a tradition concerning a historical incident intended to say as *historical tradition;* but what does matter is why it is *given to us* as a part of the word of God by virtue of a divinely directed history. For example, the original narrators of the story of the sons of God and the daughters of men (Gen. 6:1-4) or of the Tower of Babel (Gen. 11) perhaps wanted primarily only to tell their listeners something that to them was interesting and belonged to history, about the giants of ancient days, about the reason for the many languages in the world, or the reason for the ruined tower over in Babylonia. But in addition to this certainly the compilers of the source material—the Yahwist and the Elohist and perhaps already the ancient saga tellers—wanted to give examples of the human urge to transgress the limits set by God and to testify to the perversity of the human heart (Gen. 8:21). For those who wrote down the sagas this was doubtless the main point. But even if they should not have seen this as the main task, it is still *this* meaning that the stories as a whole convey as parts of the totality of Holy Writ and that draws for us the line of revelation from the ancient days through Christ to the consummation, from Genesis through the Gospels to the Revelation of John. In the purpose that *God* had for the Bible to accomplish, *this* is what these stories are meant to tell us.

The inspired authors of the Mosaic laws certainly thought that it was necessary for life and salvation to keep all these commandments concerning sacrifices and blood ceremonies, and so on, to the last point. They certainly did not think that the sacrifices were forecasts of Christ or something similar. But to the extent that they were formed by that same longing that first found its satisfaction in Christ, they *are* such temporary forecasts. Paul saw and made clear to all subsequent Christian thought and conscience that these laws were "fulfilled" and "completed" and thereby abolished in Christ. He also saw their deepest intent: to awaken the consciousness of sin and thereby lead us to Christ. In *this* sense they are still not "abolished"—they still speak of the absolute demands of God and of the folly of the human heart, which believes that it can haggle with God and satisfy him with such "sacrifices." Compare with this the prophet's attitude to sacrifice and also that of many of the psalmists (Pss. 50, 51).

That this view is correct is apparent simply from the fact that Christ is the "law," that is, the fulfillment and goal of the Old Testament. Jesus did not come to reveal history or astronomy or archaeology to us, but to reveal the Father through the Son. What we must seek in the Old Testament's traditions as links in a total revelation is what they can tell us about the Father and our relationship to him.

It is, therefore, theologically justified to let the total sweep of the Old Testament throw light upon and interpret the individual detail, even where this, historically speaking, is not the original meaning of the detail. We must assume that the scriptures are given to *us* (Rom. 15:4). And we have received the whole, not only the details. Here the purely historical, the theological, and the practical-devotional interpretation may go in different directions. To take an example: Even if the ancient stories about Jacob betray that the narrator sanctioned and enjoyed his sly tricks and did not for a moment regard what later occurred to him (in the form of trickery and treason on the part of his sons) as the fruit of his own dishonesty, we have the right to let the stories as a whole illustrate the latter insight and to use them as an expression of God's disciplinary guidance. Their close connection with the Joseph-stories also lets the Jacob-stories share the lesson that is one of the main points there, that God can transpose sin into his own positive plan: "You meant evil against me; but God meant it for good" (Gen. 50:20).

It may be asserted, therefore, that God did not give us the Bible in order to educate us as to the origin of languages, the principles of the calendar, the time of Creation, where Cain got his wife, from which people Israel was descended, and so on, but in order to show us the way to himself—the "way" that at last is revealed to be Jesus Christ.

All other things in the Bible are the form of the revelation, not its content.

32. Thus the Bible gives a creative, judging and saving revelation necessary for life and not intellectual knowledge of minutiae. On this basis it is clear in which way the Old Testament is supported by the authority of Jesus and in which way it is not. It is often said by laymen with a so-called "simple faith," in reality a primitive theology, that when Jesus said that the "Books of Moses" were written by Moses, the Psalms by David, and that the whole book of Isaiah was a work by

the prophet Isaiah, or that the story of Jonah is real history, then it must be so, for we have to accept the authority of Jesus even in such matters.

The question, however, is wrongly put. Jesus does not want to teach us about who wrote the Pentateuch or the Psalms. Jesus desires only to reveal God, to be his active, judging and saving act of revelation in the world. It is about *this* that Jesus wants to teach us, and it is to *this revelation* that all of his words exhort us to take a personally responsible stand. On anything beyond the "salvation" of the world—in the full meaning of this word—he has no special mission to us. He does not want to teach ethics, although he has something to say about morals insofar as he will create the new man within us. He does not speak of social politics, except that where he has created the new love within us, there a new policy must be the result. He does not want to teach us scientific results, neither a history of biblical literature nor a geological calendar; yet his word has a message also for science in his demand for honesty and truth. This demand he makes no less strongly of that science that professes to be the "science" about him and God, that is, theology.

When Jesus, therefore, introduces a saying with "Moses said" or "David says" (in the Psalms), it is not about the authorship of Moses or David he speaks, but about God and of us and himself. That which is guaranteed by the authority of Jesus is his revelation of God and himself and us, not a conception about the authorship of the Books of Moses or the Psalms. And when he argues in this way from the Old Testament, God, not David or Moses, is the authority; it is as word of God, not of Moses, that the Old Testament has authority for him. This is quite clear in his words concerning divorce: "For your hardness of heart Moses allowed you to divorce your wives, but from the beginning it was not so." (Matt. 19:8 ff.). The ordinance of God stands above the law of Moses. If thus the Old Testament is word of God, it is evidently of little importance to which man "the word came."

When Jesus argues from the Old Testament with his contemporaries, it is evident that he does so in the current conceptions and the terminology of his day. Since it was current practice to say, "Moses says," or "David says," Jesus naturally uses this terminology in the same sense as if he had said, "It is written in the law of Moses"; "It is written in the Psalms." He is not thereby giving any teaching as to who had written the books in question. On the contrary, he quite simply and unreflectingly took for granted that what theology in his day was saying and what he had learned at school was correct. It is rather self-evident that he shared the ideas of his contemporaries in matters like these.

If it is true that Jesus as man was as one of us except that he had no sin (Heb. 4:15), then he also shared our imperfect insight into all matters pertaining to the world of sense, the world of "science" (cf. Mark 13:32). He knew neither more nor less than most people of his class in Galilee or Jerusalem concerning history, astronomy, geography, or the history of biblical literature.

What Jesus guarantees about the Old Testament is that it is the word of God to Israel, and thereby to us. What that means we have seen above: namely, the knowledge of God's self-communicating act of judgment and salvation, mediated through the consciousness and conceptions of men.

It is this revelation that Jesus guarantees and that he himself completes.

He did not want to teach us anything about the human side of the revelation. That is the task of theological study and thinking.

One thing, however, he did say concerning the human side of scripture and the limitation of revelation by its place and time in history—namely, that these *do exist*. "For your hardness of heart Moses allowed you to divorce your wives." But it was not a command according to God's order of creation and his innermost plan and thought. Again, he said, "It is said of old, but *I* say to you."

33. If it is true that God's word of revelation is a historical entity that always has a human side, a "form" conditioned by the way of thinking and the whole level of contemporaneous culture, then it is also clear that God can and must have spoken through forms of expression that, from our standpoint of scientific knowledge of the world around us, must be called *mistakes* and *errors*. This is simply what the Bible itself says, for God can speak to us "by the mouth of babes and infants" (Ps. 8:2). God can speak even through our sins if we confess them and surrender them to his grace in Christ. There is no means too lowly to mediate the divine revelation.

Since the form of the revelation in the Old Testament is determined by the "history of its time," by ways of thinking, insights, conceptions, and terminology belonging to the time in which "the word of God was proclaimed," it also shares the limitation of its time. This has no significance for the revelational character of the Old Testament, and the fact that historical and scientific mistakes and errors can be found in the Scriptures is no cause for surprise or offense. The urge to self-glorification in the human heart is just as well illustrated by the story of the tower at Babel, even though philology tells us that languages did not arise in that way. The statement that Samaria was taken and destroyed by Shalmaneser—in reality by Sargon—is not God's word. What is intended by this inaccurately transmitted fact in its context and within the interpretation of history in which it is placed is to say that it will be thus with any people that lets itself be guided by the greed, fear, hatred, and humanly clever politics that these great powers prescribe, rather than by God. In Deut. 14, the chapter on clean and unclean animals, the genuine purpose is not to give information about a Jewish scientific attempt to classify animals, but rather to enforce and make concrete the demand for purity in daily life. Then the fact that the classification of the animals is incorrect in several respects to our present view does not matter. Incidentally the very concept of purity is still conceived of here in an external material way that has not attained the level of Christianity's concept of purity.

It is quite obvious that revelation in the Old Testament as a whole is dressed in the robe of an ancient Israelitic and Oriental primitive world-view, and that this governs its ideas, its conception of reality, and its forms of thought.

It is, for example, self-evident that the concept of God that the desert tribes were able to form has very primitive features: God is bound to nature, wild, unpredictable, "demonic," sometimes cruel. It does not surprise us to hear that they could suppose that Yahweh fell upon Moses in the night trying to kill him because he was not circumcised (Exod. 4:24-26).

Again, it is self-evident that the settlement in Canaan and the transition to the form of life of the farmer and city dweller changed the picture of God: it became more and more human, later even royal; it made the sphere of divine activity greater and placed fertility, harvest, rain, and sun under his sway. It also, however, threatened to ruin the ethics of the people by the orgiastic forms of worship that were common among the Canaanites, especially in connection with the cult of the goddess of fertility (cultus-prostitution, Gen. 38:12 ff.; I Sam. 2:22; I Kings 3:16 ff.; 15:12; Deut. 23:18 ff.; sacrifice of children, Gen. 22; Ezek. 20:25-26).

Thus it becomes easy to understand that the demand upon Abraham for complete obedience and trust could take the form of a demand to sacrifice his only son as a burnt offering to the Deity (Gen. 22).

It is natural that Yahweh only little by little is able to throw off the ties of tribe and people and land in the consciousness of the Israelites and so finally to become universal, become truly one and a truly ethical God.

There is nothing strange about the fact that the world is thought of as created in six days and in a sequence that does not harmonize with what we now know,[2] and that the history of mankind is narrowed down to an unreasonably short span of time, further that the earth is thought of as a plane resting upon pillars in the ocean with heaven as a glass bowl turned over it, the stars moving in their fixed ways over the firmament.

We should not be disturbed either by learning that the prophetic expectations concerning the future sometimes were not fulfilled, or at least not in the way that they meant, or that their expectations sometimes were influenced by what they as Jews wished to happen rather than what they should be prepared for out of the understanding of God's revelation that

[2] For instance, the light is created before the heavenly bodies that give light. It should be evident that Gen. 1 does not speak of some sort of "cosmic light" outside of the "telluric system." Its point of view is limited solely to that part of the universe that the human eye can see, with the earth as center and with sun and moon and the visible stars.

the best of them had received and tried to mediate to their disciples. We also have to accept the fact that the Old Testament "Messiah" in reality is only a shadow of that which really came in Jesus Christ, further that the gleam of light that was cast forward in the songs of the suffering Servant of Yahweh toward the true mediator of salvation was seen and accepted by very few, if any, in the Old Testament period. All of this is self-evident.

34. That the word of revelation is connected with time is most clearly expressed by the phrase "the Word became flesh." In reality this is what was happening throughout the whole history of revelation. Christ, the Word, the creative, self-giving activity of God, was also active in the Old Testament (cf. I Cor. 10:4). The word has in every period become one with a specific man in a definite concrete situation (cf. below sec. 44). Thereby it became the driving force in that man's life and strives to be so also in his environment. "The word of the Lord came" to the prophets, it is asserted; but a more correct translation of the Hebrew verb would be: "The word of the Lord became active reality with." When this happens, then it becomes one with the whole personality of the prophets, so that they then know the feelings of Yahweh, think his thoughts, have his reactions against the sin of men and their foolishness or faithfulness and obedience. Jeremiah is full of the wrath of Yahweh, and he pours it out upon great and small alike (Jer. 6:11-12). The word becomes a consuming fire in his bones and must be proclaimed (Jer. 20:7). The prophets condemn their own people against their own feelings and natural will because they can do no other (Jer. 20:7-8). Thus "the Word became flesh," flesh in Amos, flesh in Isaiah, flesh in Jeremiah, stamped with their human individual nature and situation, and yet the word of God.

In all its fullness, however, the word as God's whole activity and will became flesh in him who is called the Word, Jesus. In him God's creating and saving plan became man, came "in the likeness of sinful flesh" (Rom. 8:3), subject to all our human limitations and weaknesses, and still God's complete revelation and Word.

It is important that we try to hold on to this paradox—the Scriptures as fully human word and fully divine word—without veiling reality in any sort of unrealistic dogma of infallibility.

Word of God and words of men at the same time! The Spirit testifies with our spirit, as Paul expresses it.

It is this very viewpoint, of revelation as *inspired testimony* from God by men to whom God has revealed himself, that best throws light upon the double nature of revelation and scripture. We shall later return to the word of God as "testimony." The inspired authors were able to testify to just so much as they had seen, heard, and received. And they received just so much as they could receive according to their personal and historical circumstances. This has to be emphasized: namely, that it was *according to both their personal and their historical circumstances.*

Personal circumstances really mean: according to the degree of one's personal surrender to God. The fullness and depth of what I can receive and conceive of the "knowledge of God"—both as general understanding of God and his work and of man's relationship thereto, and also as personal re-creating appropriation of God's work and an understanding of his will and plan for my life—is dependent upon how completely I am willing to let myself go, surrender all limitations and reservations toward God, and subject myself to him in full confidence and obedience. We know, however, that there always will be something missing in this surrender, obedience, and confidence. It will ever be thus, so long as we live under human conditions. This is true of me, but also of the most perfect saint and the most inspired prophet and apostle. Absolute and perfect clarity and fullness in appropriating the depth of God's nature and wisdom does not, therefore, belong to man's situation on earth.

Now it is also true that revelation contains an intellectual aspect—a recognition of facts and relations that one must express in a form as clear and valid as possible. It is, therefore, evident that there is a difference in the amount of truth that each person is able to receive; this is determined not only by his moral character and his willingness to obey God, but also by his intellect and temperament. This is, in part, what Paul implies when he speaks of the varied gifts of the Spirit. For among these are not only the special gifts that God gave through the Spirit of Christ as supplements, so to speak, to natural endowments—prophecy, spiritual insight, healing power, and so on—but also those things that from a nonreligious viewpoint we usually call "natural endowments." This "natural" endowment is also a part of the creative work of God; and as I have pointed out, there is a positive connection between God's creating, revealing, and saving work and salvation's sequel in sanctification. Or to say it in another way: There is a unity of content among these three articles of faith; they do not express complexes of truth separated from one another but, rather, matters that stand in organic and necessary relation to one another. In the work of creation God also reveals himself, and his revelation is constantly taking place through and in connection with what he has created. That is just the reason why revelation is history, as we have seen. When in the first article of the Creed [3] we confess faith in God as the one who "has made *me* and all creatures, that He has given *me* my body and soul, eyes, ears and all my members, my reason and all my senses," then we have said that all this is part of God's plan of creation and revelation. God has created us with varieties of individual equipment, each with *his own* "reason," with *his own* peculiarities of intellect, temperament, and character, none of us having exactly the same. These differences are God-decreed basic factors that operate in all history, operate decisively, moreover, by virtue of the "once-for-all-ness" of history. The "natural" psychosomatic apparatus (our mind and brain) that God uses to get into contact with each one of us is variously individualized. This means that what each person can understand and receive from God as general or as personal revelation shows individual gradations.

To deny that revelation appears in various gradations in the various mediators of revelation in the Bible, and that it is determined as to both form and content by their individuality and their various mental and physical equipment, would in reality be to deny the first article of the Creed or, rather, to refuse to accept the consequences of that article of faith.

On the other hand, however, it becomes clear also that our "natural" endowment, "our reason and all our senses," are elements that are essential when it comes to the daily reception and use of divine guidance for our life and work. They are given us in order not to be switched out of the circuit, but to be lighted by God's spirit and so be used. Reason and revela-

[3] The Apostles' Creed as interpreted in Luther's Shorter Catechism.

tion are not opposites; neither are reason and guidance, for we are here speaking of inspired thoughts, revealed thoughts, and guided thoughts.

Secondly, however, it is also true that the mediator of revelation is influenced by his historical circumstances, by his time's general culture and insight, its ways of thinking and its horizon. All men are influenced by their social milieu and its past, even those who are ahead of their times or are breaking new paths and seeing new visions. A period, for instance, that thinks in absolutely collectivistic terms and that, like ancient Israel, can conceive of no existence for the individual outside of the tribe and the national relationship—such a time simply cannot generate the thought-forms of nineteenth-century one-sided individualism or give birth to anything like its idea of "personality." The genius—and he to whom God reveals himself—can lift the standards and extend the borders, but not beyond certain limits: not beyond the possibilities that lie latent in that specific culture and its mode of thinking. Furthermore, the new that he sees must be given form in "concepts" and idioms that can be understood by his contemporaries; otherwise he can neither think it nor express it. Language itself sets definite limits to thought. No one can reach beyond the presuppositions determined by his own historical setting. And it is within these that God's intervention takes place in his life.

Thus dependence upon history and limitations of time are placed even upon the testimony of revelation. With a certain right, therefore, we may speak, with Hempel, of "broken testimony": the light of God falls more or less "broken" through the window of human consciousness and responsiveness.

But we must look upon this "natural" relationship from a religious standpoint and see it as something willed and brought about by God. Thus we must say that the individual mediator of revelation down through the ages has been able to receive as much of the divine light as *according to God's own purpose for the course of history* he was conditioned to receive, and as much as his decree of self-surrender was willing to receive. *Why* God placed such limits and why he willed that there should be such a history of revelation and of mankind, we can never explain, beyond the quite general answer: in order to reveal "his glorious grace" (cf. Eph. 1:3-5). It is beyond the possibility of human reason to comprehend this in detail. But we are duty bound to take note that it is so and to bow before both the fact of a *history* of revelation and the limitation of that fact in time and history. We should not, therefore, show partiality toward God or be his (false) attorney, as Job says,[4] by tinkering with God's world of reality on the basis of our pet religious theories.

The revelation has come to us in a form limited by time and history. The revelation in Christ is the perfect revelation of God in regard to everything pertaining to the work of salvation and my personal acceptance of it. But even the revelation in Christ does not give perfection all at once in a complete realization of God. That is why Christ at his departure said to his disciples that he still had many things to tell them, which they could not yet understand; but he would send them the Spirit of Truth, who would guide them to all truth, according to their need and maturity.

The Old Testament and the Scriptures as a whole are "broken testimony," *God's testimony concerning himself, broken by the imperfect receiving apparatus of man, man's imperfect testi-*

[4] Job 13:8 as translated by Mowinckel himself in *Det Gamle Testamente IV,* (Skriftene, 1. del; Oslo: 1955), p. 336.

mony about what God did and has come to be for them, for us, for the world.

In spite of this we say that the Old Testament is word of God. This does not mean that every single word in some mechanical manner is God's own speech or dictation, but that God in one way or another is giving himself throughout all scripture and all its parts. We, therefore, can very well use another term and say that word of God is *in* the Old Testament, if we only remember that by that we are not saying that some of it is word of God and some not. Even the "worthless" words and thoughts for which the Lord rebukes Jeremiah (15:19) or the speeches of Job's friends for which they were rebuked by God, "for you have not spoken of me what is right, as my servant Job has" (Job 42:7)—even these have become word of God by being accepted into a whole that desires to teach us something about God in his relationship to us as "unrighteous" men.

Some will say it is too weak to say that the Old Testament is "testimony concerning revelation." This means no weakening, however. For God's revelation *is* testimony, God's testimony, namely, in work and word concerning himself; and it is men's testimony concerning the revelation because all this is received and passed on through human consciousness. Below I shall further discuss revelation as testimony. It not only is the biblical term but is really the most appropriate term to use about the word.

If the word, revelation, is at one and the same time both divine and human, then we cannot mechanically place a sign of equation between the letter of the Scriptures and the word of God. This is a theological truism. On the other hand, we have no mechanical means by which to separate something in the Old Testament as the word of God and something that is not. All is God's word and testimony concerning himself, and all is human testimony. The one in and through the other because it all is organically bound together and forms an organic history.

Only a judgment on the basis of the revelation in Christ and the testimony of the Spirit in the New Testament and in the Church, together with an honest historical study, can determine what *the word of God is for us today.*

Poetry, Secular and Sacred Legend, Myth[1]

35. From a historical viewpoint it becomes evident that God can speak through any means of expression natural to the time in question—just as he can reveal himself through any historical occurrence or person whatsoever and use them as his tools. Thus we see in the Old Testament that all human ways of thinking and speaking are used as media of revelation.

[1] Professor Mowinckel uses four Norwegian words for the superscription of this chapter: *Diktning, Sagn, Legende, Myte.* They are difficult to translate because of the shades of meaning conveyed by each one of them, and also because the English etymological equivalent to one of them has acquired another meaning.

The first, *Diktning* (cognate with the German *Dichtung*), is a wide term covering all the art of literature: poetry, fiction, and drama. Since Professor Mowinckel is here discussing only poetic expressions of *Diktning,* I have found it satisfactory to translate the word by "poetry." The content of the second term, *Sagn,* is covered by the English word "legend."

The third term, *Legende,* which is both phonetically and semantically rather close to the English word used to translate *sagn,* I prefer to translate "sacred legend."

The fourth term, *Myte,* borrowed from Greek, is equivalent to its English fellow loanword "myth." (Translator's note.)

From the New Testament we know that Jesus conveyed some of his deepest revelations in the parables, stories that he composed. In the Old Testament, too, inspired poetry is a means of revelation, a link in the history of revelation. We have only to recall *the Psalms.* They are conceived, created, and sung as words of men in distress or as thanksgiving and worship. But as the mind is turned toward God and the combined emotion, thought, and will seek him with all the ability that the person in question has at his command at that time, and with the will to surrender conditioned by his disposition and life, the ideas and words of the prayer become guided thoughts and words that open our minds to a deeper insight into the being, will, and plan of God. God is near to them who seek him, and in his Spirit he is always present with those who pray honestly. This is true also for the Old Testament men of prayer, so that even if in their limited ability, will, moral level of development, and willingness to surrender they often do not know what to pray for, the Spirit himself intercedes for them and often makes their words proleptic—spoken "ahead of their natural time," so to speak. The Old Testament Psalms were perhaps in most cases not given form by the person who first used them. They were given poetic form for use in the typical situations of worship, but out of a concrete singular event and probably in most cases by one of the sanctuary's own worship personnel.[2] It is self-evident, however, that even in his hands they were given form out of the poet's personal relationship to God and out

[2] On this point see S. Mowinckel, *Psalmenstudien VI. Die Psalmdichter.* Videnskapsselskapets Skrifter. II Hist. Filos. Kl. 1924. No. 1, Oslo. Cf. also Aage Bentzen, *Introduction to the Psalms of the Old Testament* (Copenhagen: C. E. Gad, 1948). Mowinckel, *Offersang og Sang-offer* (Oslo: Aschehoug & Co., 1951). E. A. Leslie, *The Psalms, Translated and Interpreted in the Light of Hebrew Worship* (Nashville: Abingdon Press, 1949).

of his parallel experiences in similar situations. The psalmists, therefore, spoke not only for themselves but also for all pious believers in a similar situation, even though the psalmists' conscious spiritual horizon did not reach any further than to the borders of Israel. When a man and his prayer are one, then God speaks. Man's prayer becomes inspired prayer, guided prayer. So when the psalmists speak in the name of all individuals, their expressions for distress, prayer and confidence in God and surrender, thanksgiving, and worship so often have a universal character and express a view of God that in its consequences reaches further than they themselves realized. When their view of God is seen in the light of the revelation in Jesus Christ, they spoke truer than they themselves could know. The Psalms in this way become at the same time both man's prayer and God's revelation.

Another classical example of poetry as a medium of revelation is the *poem of Job*.[3] That this work is a poem and not a historical work recording the conversations of the friends is apparent from the form alone. The four friends, of whom one is even sick unto death, quite evidently did not sit talking to one another in verses of regular meter and form. Such speech is that of a poet, who wants to reach truth about the religious problem that occupies him with all the means that are available to him. Job then is a religious poem on a familiar problem. Its theme is the problem of the suffering of a righteous man, which arises for the poet out of the tension between real experience and the common belief of his day that there was an outward mechanical balance between piety and happiness, ungodliness and suffering. Thus it really is the problem of the righteous-

[3] Emil Kraeling, *The Book of the Ways of God* (New York: Charles Scribner's Sons, 1938).

ness of God. The poem emerges from a deeper view of piety and human sinfulness than the common mechanical doctrine of retribution of the day. The poet has received a clearer view from God concerning the problem and its solution than his contemporaries have. The Old Testament here again breaks with one of its earlier levels of development. The poet does not give a logical solution to his problem. What he has seen, however, is an important point on the line that leads through the concept of the suffering servant of the Lord in Isa. 53 forward to Christ: namely, that the problem cannot be solved logically but only by a confident and willing surrender to God's righteousness, goodness, and omnipotence. According to the general Old Testament view, God's righteousness, power, and wisdom are one and the same thing. The poet surrenders humbly to God's superior power and wisdom. He finds a convincing testimony to this in the wonders of nature, and their very opacity testifies to him of a wisdom higher than all human reason. There are still, however, facts that cannot be explained away. This gives Job the courage to trust that the wisdom of God and his righteousness are dominant also in human life, even where our eye cannot see or understand them. God is God, and his essence in spite of everything is righteousness. This is a law guiding and upholding the world, even if human destinies are crushed and we do not understand why. Thereby that which the friends maintain also becomes correct, but in a deeper way than they see it: that is, that over against God man is never in the right—he is always condemned by God's purity. Thus also Job points forward to the atonement in Christ. The poem, therefore, is inspired, guided understanding—a "word" from God in the form of a poem. Compared with this, it is a matter of complete indifference whether or not a man named Job ever existed.

36. In view of such insights it should be evident that the understanding of God's thoughts—that is, his word and revelation—also may be given in other poetic forms, as, for instance, in secular and sacred legend. People, in general, still think of these terms as equivalent to fable, fairy tale, or falsehood. This is completely wrong and shows only the inability of present-day man to understand the modes of thought and speech belonging to other times and other forms of culture. Secular "legend"—the word means etymologically the same as "saga" (that which is "said," passed on by oral tradition)—is not false but is a certain way of seeing and saying a reality and trying to explain it. Sacred legend—which etymologically signifies the stories of the lives of saints, which "are to be read" in worship on the day of each saint—in the terminology of folklore-research is used of traditions that have a religious, edifying content. Of both types of legend it is true that reality is seen with primitive thought's eye for the picturesque, or through the poetic spectacles with which the childlike mind sees all reality. Consequently the legend has definite distinguishing marks as to style and content. It is reality in the form of poetry. To that extent we may call it pictorial speech. It lays hold of a reality that it wants to preserve and explain to those who are affectively interested in it. The legend thus always has a realistic "core" of some sort.

In the Old Testament we could be tempted to speak of *sacred legends,* for it must be said concerning the ancient Israelitic-Jewish legends that the total view of life that determines them is always a religious one. They speak of a reality in which man always senses and sees the Divine behind the wonders of nature and life. In addition they have gone through that sifting process that is the divinely guided history of the Canon (see below). Secular material or material of low religious grade was to a large extent sifted out of the tradition.

I have mentioned above a few examples of revelational truths in the form of legend (the Tower of Babel and the ancient giants). I would like to discuss here a little more closely a few more. First, the story of the Fall (Gen. 3). It is characterized by the pictorial language of legend. God, so to speak, walks about in person in the Garden, cooling himself in the afternoon breeze; he makes with his own hands clothes of skin for man; the serpent speaks; the fruit of a tree gives knowledge and wisdom; the "flaming sword" stands as a doorkeeper at the gate of paradise. All these are conceptions gathered from the childhood of mankind with its fantasies about ancient times, about a golden age, a land of gods and fairyland, about supernatural beings, and so on. But these stories also represent reflections about some of man's elementary and basic questions—the attraction between the sexes, the contrast between carefree and stupid childhood and strenuous and wise adulthood, the pangs of childbirth, the poverty of the earth and the struggle for daily bread, age and disease and the decay of the body in death. In this handed-down oral tradition deep reflections were already expressed. The inspired storyteller, however, who out of this material created the legend as we have it, saw something that belongs to man's essence and is the explanation for all his misery: sin. And he saw the true nature of sin—disobedience to the plan of God, a disobedience founded upon self-assertion, greed, and arrogance. This disobedience turns inward and creates in us an uneasy conscience. It generates embarrassment, self-isolation, restraint, anxiety, excuses, lies, the urge to blame others, defiance, despair—in short, it erects all those insurmountable walls of division between man and his God and between man and his fellow man that are the cause for his misery. The disobedience may be petty, childish; but in essence it is always itself. And its consequences are inescapable. The storyteller knows that this is the way we all are, but that God cannot have created us this way. In childlike form but actually deeply and in utter moral seriousness he has faced the problem of evil and the origin of suffering. He came to the point to which even modern thinking constantly returns when this problem becomes acute: namely, to the insight that it must have been at a certain specific time and with a certain specific person that this conflict between a higher destiny and a conscious compliance with the downward pull came to a conscious crisis—the problem of the fall of man. So he gave form to this story, which gives that answer that God had led him to see for all these problems. It is easy to see that the answer is universally valid. Thus every man experiences the Fall anew, the conscious victory of egoism over God's destiny for us, the "image of God" within us. This is the Fall to which we are destined by "inheritance and environment"—"original sin"—which we nevertheless experience as our own "guilt"—our personal guilt. How deeply he sees the connection among the various forms of selfish desire. How well he sees the connection between man's intellectual awakening and his sexuality, the connection between sex, which in itself is good and holy, and the selfish lust of the Fall, with its consciousness that sin is the loss of something that can never be regained! How universally valid his description of the psychology of sin is—from the first playful thought about it on to the Fall, the denial, and the defiance, and finally the collapse or the resignation when the unavoidable consequence comes. In the form of legend the God-inspired truth about man is asserted about the first man as well as the last, about me and about you. It is the same truth into which Paul has seen ever deeper in his confession "The good that I would I do not. But the evil which I would not, that I do" (Rom. 7:19 K.J.V.).

The author who first put this story into a larger context, a saga of the origin of mankind, is the "Yahwist." [4] In the popular traditions he also found a few other legends that were able to illustrate the idea that he had got as the leitmotiv for his saga: the idea of man's insane tendency to transgress his limits, and of what God consequently must do in order that "the trees should not grow into heaven." The first of these concerns the *origin of the giants* (Gen. 6:1 ff.). Almost all peoples have legends about ancient giants; it is the way in which they explain the existence of such "gigantic" remains as colossal graves or Cyclopean walls. These giants must have been semigods, for such buildings can no longer be built! So they tell the legend of how the "sons of God," that is, the supernatural beings, married daughters of men and with them produced the giants. They also told such stories in Israel, probably after the model of the Canaanites. These stories the "Yahwist" took up and transformed into divine understanding. A new proof of men's pride! But also, however, an example of the heavy charge in the battery of their minds! The Divine and the human are at war within them. There is something grand even in this untamed urge to break and move boundaries. As an ancient Hebrew the "Yahwist" cannot help admiring the tribe of Lamech, the honor of which

[4] Cf. an introduction to the Old Testament, for instance, Robert Pfeiffer, *Introduction to the Old Testament* (New York: Harper & Bros., 1941), pp. 142 ff. Also Bentzen, *op. cit.*, II, pp. 44 ff.

is so great that it must be revenged seven times seventy-seven (Gen. 4:23-24). But the idea that he places in our hand, so to speak, is this: What this urge could do if it were willing to place itself under the control of God! Ancient Israel actually did have this idea, for it is dawning in the book of Judges in the stories of the "heroes" (inaccurately called "judges" in the English Bible) who are driven to mighty deeds by the "Spirit of Yahweh."

In the legend about the giants, however, this does not consciously come out. In the Yahwist's text it provides a transition to the next, the legend about the *Tower of Babel,* which illustrates the same thought but also shows the consequences: The untamed arrogance and covetousness, the naïve self-confidence and egoism and the urge to self-assertion are in reality the cause of the eternal estrangement and conflict that alienate races, peoples, and individuals from one another, waste their powers, and make it impossible to build a really shared and sharable home on this earth. Is there any truth more necessary for our time to face up to than this? And when will the proofs we have for it be enough to convince us? One culture after another has fallen into dust. Not even so much as the ruins of that proud Tower of Babel remains to remind us of some of them. Yet there is one single cause for it all: human sin and folly—of individuals, classes, peoples, and kingdoms.

The younger of the two ancient saga writers, the "Elohist," [5] also began with the story of Creation and paradise. As proof of the inherited evil of man he told the *legend of the great Flood,* which Israel in the meantime had learned about from Babylonia-Assyria. As an example of how the human heart is wicked

[5] Cf. *ibid.,* pp. 168 ff.

from its youth onward, he told the story of Cain and Abel.[6]

The revelation—word of God—in this story is not historical-archaeological information concerning names, locations, occupations, and the mutual relationships of the first men—it is the business of science to find out such things. Rather, the revelation here is a divinely guided personal acknowledgment of the native wickedness of the heart: that envy is the root of murder, and that envy, hatred, violence, and vindictiveness have from the very first ruined relationships between persons who were made to live together as brothers, and that they will continue to do so if we do not let God have dominion over our lives.

Now let us look at the story of the *sacrifice of Isaac* (Gen. 22). The Norwegian newspapers once ran a story about a teacher who had tried to tell his pupils that even our understanding of God and ethics is subject to the law of change, and that it was according to the beliefs of a bygone era that Abraham was able to believe that God demanded of him that he sacrifice his son. A minister more zealous than wise publicly interfered with this instruction and demanded that the teacher stick to the Book, for there it is written that it was God who wanted to test Abraham.[7]

[6] This distribution of the stories of the ancient history between J and E is not the common one. I have tried to show that this is right in my *The Two Sources of the Predeuteronomic Primeval History (JE) in Genesis 1-11* (Avhandlinger utgitt av Det Norske Videnskapsakademi i Oslo. II Hist.-Filos. Klasse 1937. No. 2) Oslo: 1937. (The author wants to add that he has become very doubtful in regard to "E" as a thoroughgoing literary "source." He is now much more inclined to take "E" as a gradual transformation of the same traditions that had been put in writing by "J." The oral tradition goes on beside and in spite of its literary fixation. Translator's note.)

[7] It should be remembered here that there is a Lutheran State Church in Norway, and that religion is taught in the public schools as part of the curriculum. A Lutheran minister, therefore, feels an obligation as a public official to defend what he believes to be the faith. (Translator's note.)

The minister was correct in his last assertion, but the important thing is that one try to see what was really meant. It is quite evident that God cannot "test" a man of faith by giving him an idea (a "word" of God) that flatly commands him to do something that he directly knows is wrong and contrary to that understanding of God and the moral law that he already has. Compare this with what was said above about the prophets. Their most important touchstone for knowing whether the word that came to them really was the Lord's or not, for instance, a word from Baal or some other kind of diabolic inspiration, was the question whether the word could measure up to that ethical view of God that their "knowledge of God" had revealed to them. It is further clear that we must think of testings from God not as direct voices from heaven or the like, but rather as an incentive, a stimulus, which in Abraham's case came to him in the same way in which "God's word" is usually considered to come in the Old Testament. It may be as an inner voice, an emergent idea, or it may be the interpretation of an oracle. It is impossible that Abraham could have understood the exhortation to go and sacrifice his son as a command from God, if his understanding of God had not still been such that he could suppose a person might be worshiping God, doing him a "service," by sacrificing human beings to him. Only such a supposition could make the thought a real test of obedience.

This story desires to achieve two things. It does not actually contain any protest against child sacrifice per se, but contains rather an abrogation of it. God *can* demand anything, even *that;* but he is so good and full of grace toward the obedient and pious that he does not do it. He does not test them beyond capacity. The main purpose of the story, however, is to tell about confident obedience to God—how necessary it is and how it opens the way to freedom and blessing. We all know from experience that we are enslaved, bound, and unhappy so long as we have not been able to surrender our last reservations toward God. We also know that we do not find truly secure freedom, true release from all fear and feelings of impotence, from all unrest and a half-clean conscience, until the moment when we let go of ourselves and cast ourselves upon him and say an unreserved "yes" to God and declare ourselves willing to do, by his help, all he may demand of us even though it be in fear and trembling. At the very moment we let him give us the ability and willingness to say this "yes," we also experience the feeling: You may say "yes" to him in all confidence, for God wills no evil. God demands of us nothing but what is good for us. God demands no more of us than he gives us strength for—if each time we only dare to cast ourselves upon him. It is this constraint that is real freedom.

This is what the story of Abraham, when clearly seen, wants to express. Each of us can come to a position in which obedience to God, the call he has given us or the actual task that he has placed before us, demands that we give up that which is dearest to us. Indeed, the decisive Christian transition from death to life, from sin to grace, from chaos to a divinely guided life, is concentrated into such a demand: Here life and death are at stake—mine!—and I *may* not take anything else into consideration. Therefore, Jesus can speak the apparently merciless words: "If any one comes to me and does not hate his own father and mother and wife and children and brothers and sisters, yes, and even his own life, he cannot be my disciple" (Luke 14:26). Such words make us ask: "Who then can be saved?" But that is where Jesus answers: "With men this is impossible, but with God all things are possible" (Matt. 19:25 ff.).

The Abraham story also tells us something else. Do that single little deed of emancipating obedience and say, even though with a heart full of anxiety and reluctance: "I am willing, O Lord, help my unwillingness"—and at that moment God's re-creating, liberating power will be there, and you will see that God is love! Your "sacrifice" in this case is no bloody offering, a purposeless waste of values, but has a positive meaning and becomes a blessing to all. Then one experiences that he who loses his life shall find it (Matt. 16:25), and often also that that which is sacrificed is received back in a much truer and fuller way as a gift from God.

The story is a legend of the kind called etiological sanctuary-legend, for it has a third purpose: namely, to explain why exactly "this place" (probably Jerusalem) is a holy place for worship and why Yahweh does not demand human sacrifices here. This type of poetic explanation for a known fact is typical of the legend. But it is, so to speak, only the outside of the story and is irrelevant for the question of what in it is God's word to us. In any case, the man who formed it had experienced what it means to be confronted by the absolute demand of God and to be led to say "yes" to it. Consequently this story, too, is a masterpiece of psychological description such as only one having a personal testimony about such a surrender can tell. The storyteller here testifies in inspired words of that which he has experienced with God, that which God has shown to him when God revealed Himself to his soul. Abraham and his only son and the demand to sacrifice him as a burnt offering, the story of the founding of the Jerusalem sanctuary, then, is the known material he has at hand to illustrate what he experienced in a way that all could understand.

Precisely this open and unconditional admission of the historical independence and limitation of revelation and its records, or this distinction between their historically "accidental" form and their religio-ethical, ever-valid content, is what gives us insight—both into the revelatory character of these stories and into their value for instruction—not only their usefulness, but also their indispensability. It should not be impossible for a teacher who himself knows God to make children understand what is real and relevant for them today in these stories. But by insisting on the letter of their texts and refusing to see both their distance from Christianity and their connection with it, one gains nothing but rather causes harm.

37. And now a few words about mythology [8] in the Old Testament, in revelation. Myth likewise reflects a reality that is expressed in the pictorial language of primitive thinking and its view of reality. It differs from the legend, however, by concentrating upon the innermost, highest and deepest realities of life and existence, upon divine reality, upon that which is experienced as holy and divine. Genuine myth was originally connected with the cultus, with the creative experiences that

[8] The positive view that I briefly indicate in this section I have developed in conscious contrast to the so-called "school of comparative religion." I have previously been maintaining it in my study of the "Enthronement Psalms" and the cultus feast in Israel and of the origin of Old Testament eschatology concepts in my book *Psalmenstudien II. Das Thronbesteigungsfest Jahves und der Ursprung der Eschatologie*. Kristiania: 1922 (Videnskapsselskapets Skrifter. II kl. 1921. No. 6). I was also at that time aware of the fact that such a view of myth can be united with, and in reality is also demanded by, a historical view of revelation and a realistic biblical faith in God. See also Mowinckel, *Religion und Kultus* (Göttingen: Vandenhoeck & Ruprecht. 1953), pp. 94 ff.

the fellowship (the group, the tribe, the congregation) shares through the sacred group acts whose purpose was to actualize the connection between the divine and the human. Myth expresses the reality that is in and above those experiences in the definite idiom or a definite mentality and a definite level of culture. We are here concerned with what is called "mythical thinking" as such, a certain way of seeing, conceiving, and thinking reality. It not only embraces what we call "personification"—ascribing life to everything, even objects of nature —but is also a necessary way of expressing metaphysical experiences and realities in fanciful, epical-dramatic form. It is not, therefore, bound to the "primitive" level of development but must be used at all times when it comes to the realities of religion. When we want to talk about God and his work, matters that are really ineffable, then we often have to use the mythical form. We, therefore, may speak of myth as "pictorial language." This does not mean, however, the use of consciously comparative imagery. Myth is concerned with realities that cannot otherwise be expressed. Narrative myth expresses the truth of cultic experiences in the pictorial language of childlike mentality, but often with a piercingly keen insight into innermost reality and with such deep thoughts that any age may recognize its deepest experiences and highest truths in them. It is, however, compelled to use the imagery of naïve thinking, for we are here concerned with the experiences that are literally unspeakable, with the "innermost," "deepest," "highest" (these words are also mythology!) realities for which language is not adapted. For language is the working instrument of everyday reality, the reality of the senses.

Myth thus is a way of saying the truth. Mythology is not a derogatory word. It is a complete misunderstanding of the word when one brushes something aside by saying it is mythology—with a tacitly understood "only" before it. It is also a misunderstanding to believe that one needs to defend the Old Testament against the "accusation" that it contains mythology. It would be sad if it did not, if it presented abstract ideas instead of mythologically expressed concrete realities.

Myth thus speaks of the reality that is experienced in worship. But we know that what is experienced in worship gatherings—both in the primitive ones and in those on the highest level, even the Christian ones—may be of various sorts. We—men of all ages—can sit and experience the mystical movements of our own souls and our oneness with the universe and so deify *this.* Or we can experience fellowship and the security and joy of it and a swelling sense of power, the "soul" of the group, and deify *this.* God *may* also be in *it,* but we then confine within what is our own—or we do not let him in as he really is (either figure can be used) —and only get hold of a little fringe of his garment. We have ideas about him that are too petty, and we are not willing to let him show himself greater than our thoughts and demands. We still stand on a primitive level—where among other ways we also experience him in sacrificial slaughter, vapors of blood and ecstatic orgy, and so on, as the Israelites did in their earliest times.

It may, however, be a meeting with the real God himself that we experience in our worship-cultus, God coming with his judgment upon us and his forgiveness of sins, grace, restoration, and re-creating power. But our own cultus is one out of a wide variety and is only more or less pure according to the historical and personal stage of development upon which we stand.

Myth proper is narrative about the reality thus experienced. Here even we who are grounded in modern thought and its conception of reality must also resort to "images" because that which is to be said is ineffable, for what are terms such as "God is my Father," "God loves me," "Christ is God's Word and thought (logos)," other than mythical expressions—"images" from human relationships transferred to a reality of a completely different nature—a reality for which our terms are not adapted? In a wider sense, therefore, we use the word "mythological" for such formulations (usually in narrative form) of religious realities and thoughts as are made in the image-making terms of "mythical thinking."

There will always be basic Christian realities and thoughts that can be expressed only in mythological form, if they are to have power and clarity. Such an idea, for instance, is the *belief in creation.* What it means, a vitally important thing for us to grasp, is belief that God is a being essentially different from all that is created, but that this creation still has its life from him and, therefore, reflects him, that he is highly exalted above it but still is its Lord and "intervenes" in its smallest detail, and that our own existence is completely determined by this reality. The belief in creation is a plastic, concrete expression of this reality; and it has found its necessary form in a creation *story* of one type or another, determined by the circumstances of a particular culture, geography, and history. It is evident that these are mythical. To say this is only to say that they exist. In the biblical creation stories—there are at least two of them —the people of revelation have given their form to this idea and faith. We can make no new one because mythical thinking is no longer so immediate and consistent with us as with the people of old. It would also be unnecessary. God has given us the Bible's *forms* of this faith, and our task is to acknowledge them for what they are and to let them speak to us in the language of poetry about faith in God's power of creation, which we have to accept and build our faith upon.[9]

It is, therefore, incorrect to advocate the removal of such stories from religious education on the ground that they are mythological. They are needed to give to the idea that concrete form that is natural to children. They have only to be correctly explained—as religion, not as natural science. It is, therefore, also unnecessary to resort to such artificial reinterpretations as have so often been attempted with the creation story by saying that the six days mean geological periods, or that an earthquake coincided with the blowing of the trumpets and destroyed the walls of Jericho. If one accepts legend and myth as necessary forms of tradition and, therefore, also of revelation, such dishonest tampering falls away by itself.

It is also both unnecessary and incorrect to react against mythology by defending the Old Testament against it and trying to prove that the religion of Israel was "antimythological." This is quite clear when we see the third form of belief in creation that we meet in the prophets and the poets. With them the original primeval sea that existed before creation, the chaos before the cosmos, was a dragon that Yahweh fought with sword and bow and conquered or crushed, and built the world out of it.[10] This is more than poetical imagery—for the poets of the Psalms it was reality—and it truly is when correctly understood as the mythical expression for God's perennial creation, his working, struggling world dominion, the realization of his plan for the world. That these, however, are

[9] Cf. Alan Richardson, *Preface to Bible-Study*, pp. 75 ff.

[10] See Pss. 74:12-17; 89:10-15; 18:16 ff.; 40:5; 104:5-9, 25-26; Job 7:12; 9:13; 12–13; 38:8-12; Isa. 51:9-10; 50:2-3; 59:15-20; Hab. 3:8; Nah. 1:4. There are allusions elsewhere also.

mythically conceived realities is unquestionable; the Babylonian model for these conceptions is well known, and the dependence is obvious. For Israel the acceptance of this mythical form at that time meant a richer, more concrete understanding of the idea of creation in all its implications, a widening of their understanding of Yahweh's power and glory. It is significant that we meet it precisely in those prophets who clearly grasp faith in the one true God and make Yahweh's dominion absolute by combining the idea of creation with the idea of Yahweh as Lord of history.

Myth, however, may have higher and lower forms, may work with purer or with less pure religious and ethical concepts. This is completely dependent upon what type of religion it belongs to and wants to express, and whether *that* religion stands high or low in its understanding of God. Therefore, one of the lines in the history of revelation, in the religious development of Israel, is that the lower forms of myth are successively thrown out. God so clearly became a moral and spiritual God for the Israelitic mediators of revelation that a reaction arose against excessively anthropomorphic and ethically questionable forms of myth. So myth in the Old Testament is after all something other than "pagan" myths in spite of the fact that it has borrowed its form from them. It is hallowed myth, purified myth, myth that mediates revelation. In this sense it may be said that the religion of Israel is "antimythological."

It is significant, therefore, that there is left only a brief and eroded notice of the myth of the sons of God and the daughters of men, regardless of whether it was the Yahwist himself or some redactor who shortened the story. In his narrative account of creation the Elohist has not included the poetic variant (the fight with the dragon), even though it certainly was known in his day. In the third and youngest of the saga sources, the Priestly Document, which stands completely upon the ground of Babylonian "science" in maintaining that before creation there was sea not desert, the dragon fight is a pale memory to be read only between the lines. Only a comparative study of folklore can detect its marks; the common reader will not notice it, and the Priestly writing itself was hardly aware of it. Here the myth has become the expressive form of religious and scientific thought, both for religious faith in creation and as an attempt toward a scientifically systematized view of the origin of the world, in the same way as the oldest Ionic (Greek) philosophy of nature sprang from the struggle of thought with the ancient myths about the genesis of things.[11]

By the help of a modern theological watchword one can say that the Old Testament history of revelation itself has undertaken a certain "demythologization" [12] of the old naïvely mythological material. This took place gradually, when it was no longer felt to be a direct and proper expression for the growing religious understanding and for a more rational, ethical, and spiritual view of God. If one by "demythologization" means that Christian preaching in order to reach modern men must express Christian truths in concepts and terms which are not too intimately connected with the world views of a past era, but by terms which better harmonize with our own time, then there is really no reason to take exception from such re-

[11] This, for instance, is quite clear when the first of the philosophers, Thales from Miletus, maintained that water was the origin of all things; the connection with Babylonian-Syrian mythology is evident.

[12] Cf. R. Bultmann, *Jesus Christ and Mythology* (New York: Charles Scribner's Sons, 1958). G. W. Davis, *Existentialism and Theology* (New York: Philosophical Library, 1957). Fr. Gogarten, *Demythologizing and History* (New York: Charles Scribner's Sons, 1955).

writing. The form of the myth, however, is a medium of expression which religion can never be without. It is much more adequate than abstract philosophical ideas. Common experience also will substantiate that the deeper a person penetrates into the secrets of religion—which for us means Christianity—the more he will feel himself in need of a useful way of expressing the unspeakable, "what no eye has seen, nor ear heard, nor the heart of man conceived," and he will employ again the mythical form. On the basis of experience I can say that when we have to deal with a seeking "modern" man, "demythologizing" may be a useful pastoral tool. But as things open up for the seeker and he decides to choose the "way," then the old mythological forms of expression will appear again as the best interpreters of reality. All religious form is more or less symbolic. What, for example, would Christian hymnology do without the "mytho-poetic" forms, images, and symbols?

The Canon as Revelation

38. If Old Testament history and its continuance in the New Testament is God's history of revelation in a special sense, then the fact that we received the *compilation of these* Scriptures (the Canon, that is, the *Bible*) is also a link in this history guided by God.

In this context I am speaking only of that Old Testament that the Church took over from Judaism as a relatively closed sacred compilation. The Church knew itself to be the new Israel, the universal Israel, which was the purpose and the goal of the election and the decline of Israel as a nation. It also knew that the Scriptures of revelation applied to this new Israel—and had as their purpose to create and serve it.

It is true to say of the Old Testament and of the Scriptures as a whole that they are the milestones in the line of historical revelation that lead to and finally are realized in Christ and the New Covenant. The Old Testament together with the New Testament—thus the Bible as a whole—shows us what God has done for the salvation of the world, and also what we must learn to know about ourselves before we can see and be willing and able to understand and receive this salvation.

The Old Testament is, therefore, a testimony that has an effective relevance of its own here and now—which I shall discuss below. This is really why we have it at all: in order that it may say something to us today, saying it through these testimonies about the reality and the results of historical revelation. Just as little as it has to tell us about cosmology or cosmogony or such things do we have it for historical documentation as such; we do have it because this history has something to say to us. Therefore, its arrangement is only in part historical; the essential reality of the testimony is its spiritual content.

On the other hand, however, we may also venture to say that when the material of such a history of revelation is arranged with so little historicity, when sources of very different dates are worked together, sometimes strikingly mingled in one and the same book, and when there are so many things about which we learn so little, then all this has a positive meaning too. It confronts the Church and its theological thinking with a task: to continue constant work on the historical problems themselves. Thereby theology is constantly forced back to the living, concrete life that constituted the history, and that originated the words of revelation and was influenced by them later again. It is proper and according to the will of God that historical work with the Bible never ceases, never leads to indisputable results for every question. This is no defect in historical (critical) theology and inquiry. On the contrary, that is its honor, its right to exist because that is what invariably forces it to go back to the "sources," that is, the living life. The shortsighted man will reproach historical-critical theology because it has so few certain "results" that can be popularized for the student or the layman; instead one should be happy for this and thank God for it. "Biblical theology," historical inquiry into the Scriptures, must always be ready to discard its old results and accept new ones; "every *scribe* who has been trained for the kingdom of heaven is like a householder who brings out of his treasure what is new and what is old" (Matt. 13:52). A "scribe," a theologian, who is not willing to learn something new even though he may not like it and even though his habitual feelings and habits of thinking resist it is no scribe "trained for the kingdom." Defending old theological "truths" is not theology. Neither are old theological truths improved when they are presented as "simple lay theology," even if this be done in the best of faith.

39. But now we must ask: Is it really the significant points in the historical line forward to Christ that we are given in the scriptures and stories of the Old Testament? Is there not much inferior material, especially from a Christian standpoint? Why, for instance, is the book of Esther with its Jewish patriotic thirst for vengeance included? And why so many sections in the prophetic books that breathe the same spirit? One may also widen this question to the New Testament and ask: why do we have the Revelation of John with its fantastic imagery? or II Peter, which to a large extent is only a copy of the Letter of Jude?

We first have to answer: because God wanted it so. We cannot make over his history. History made this canon by which the Church has lived.

Our task is to ask honestly and sincerely what God wants to say to us in the sections at which we take offense. What is the meaning, for instance, of the book of Esther or of the not-so-few sections in the prophetic books in which the disciples of the prophets, men less dedicated and less sensitive to God and his will, have made additions and corrections in a spirit of nationalistic, particularistic Jewish patriotism and simply broken the edge of the sharp word of doom spoken by the prophet? The first thing we must watch is that we do not cheat by trying to reinterpret, putting other meanings into the texts than those they really have.[1] They are to be taken exactly as they are. Both the book of Esther and the prophetic redactors have to be taken seriously and placed in their right niche in the historical development of the people of Israel and thereby in the history of revelation. They then show—and this is the second point—how great or how small a distance the people, or parts of it, had then come in their understanding of the divine truths and in their willingness to grasp the meaning of God's guidance in history. They also show what type of human material God has to create and transform in order to reach his goal. They thereby say something very essential about human nature and hence about us. They show that our selfishness as individuals and groups may hide itself in traditional piety and religiosity, show us how we always involuntarily—just like those redactors of the prophets—reinterpret God's word and thoughts and wishes. They show how reluctant we all are to let God break and transform our natural selfish instincts—and why at last Christ had to die upon a cross in order to save us, since even our piety is not of any better sort.

40. Here it seems appropriate to say something about the so-called "nongenuine" passages in the Old Testament. Many im-

[1] As, for instance, W. Vischer does in his *Esther* (Theologische Existenz Heute, Heft 48), München: Kaiser Verlag, 1937. The same is true by and large for all of Vischer's treatment of Old Testament writings; it is arbitrary eisegesis and reinterpretation and, therefore, objectively dishonest.

mediately repudiate any suggestion that such may exist in the Bible, saying that to reckon with such a possibility is to practice a faith-less theology.

To this we first must say that the expression "nongenuine" in this case is very misleading; the concern here is not whether they are "genuine" or "spurious," but to distinguish which periods the various sections in a biblical book come from, that is, to distinguish the older from the younger. There is no way to avoid the conclusion that one and the same book may contain sections from various times. For instance, the second part of the book of Isaiah, chs. 40-66, comes from a quite different period and a different person than does the main part of chapters 1-39. This is a truth generally recognized by theology everywhere and is as certain as anything can be, if anything at all can be proved in the field of literary and mental history. That the other prophetic books may also contain matter from various times is, therefore, something that one must expect and not be disturbed about. It is not a matter of belief nor of unbelief, but is a question of one's ability to be discriminating in the fields of history, literature, and revelation.

The "critics" in reality do the understanding of historical revelation a great favor by such discrimination, for they actually give it a much richer selection of sources and signposts through which to draw the "line," and thereby make a much more richly shaded picture of the history of revelation and the religious life of the inspired men. The distinction between an "Isaiah" and a "Second Isaiah"—recently more and more scholars also reckon with "Third Isaiah" (chs. 56-66)—is far from meaning loss; it means, on the contrary, that we get acquainted with one or two more spirited and original prophets than we previously knew we possessed in the Old Testament.

From this viewpoint the editorial additions and modifications and the more or less appropriate explanations that have become a part of the Bible manuscripts find their meaning and value. These, too, are testimonies about men who wanted to seek the plan of God and with whom God was in contact, even though at times they were not so willing, as the older prophets of doom, to discard their customs and prejudices in order to accept his guidance. These men likewise belong both to the historical picture of reality and to the human material that God creates and through which—or in spite of which—he works.

If on the basis of one's faith in God one really believes in historical revelation through inspired men and women guided by God, then it also is an evident fact that the literary-critical question of "genuine" or "nongenuine" has nothing to do with the question of "inspired" or "not inspired." Literary criticism, that is, inquiry into the history of a literature asks, for instance, whether a given chapter is by Isaiah or by some other inspired author. The question whether it is inspired or not is decided by the fact that it is in the Canon and thereby is a link in the special historical revelation. But we always have to remember: inspired is not the same as outwardly infallible. Even the inspired word has its significance as a link in an organic historical connection, not as detached "information."

41. Instead of discussing whether something is to be cut out of the Canon, or of feeling as if criticism had taken something out of it, there may be more point in asking whether the Protestant churches have not made a mistake in gradually cutting the ties between the so-called "canonical" and the so-called "apocryphal" writings of the Old Testament; for the Apocrypha belonged to Paul's Bible, the early Church's Greek Septuagint, and there are many indications that they were authoritative writings in the circles in which Jesus grew up and by which, humanly speaking, his mind was formed. The Roman Catholic Church, therefore, has maintained that the Apocrypha, too, are inspired writings, and it has even widened the concept of inspiration to include the official Latin translation, the Vulgate.

The line of historical revelation actually goes from the Old Testament to the New Testament through the apocalyptics and the Apocrypha. To mention a single item, it is here that we find the real background for Jesus' idea of "the Son of man"; it cannot be derived directly from the Old Testament and is not understandable except against the background of the Jewish apocalypses (in English usually included among the pseudepigrapha).

The separation of the Apocrypha from the Bible in Protestant churches is really caused by a worldly humanistic attitude disguised in the cloak of the dogma of inspiration. It began with Jerome and his interest in the Hebrew root form of the Bible (*veritas hebraica*), and it continued through the Renaissance to Luther and the Reformers. However, this attitude is without real historical foundation. The tendency within Palestinian Judaism that limited the Old Testament, for Jews, to its (and our) "canonical" books was its rabbinistic petrification, not that other tendency that provided the transition to Christianity.

The Relationship to the Other Religions

42. History is the place of God's revelation, the arena of his creative mediation of himself. In the Old Testament we see the special line of revelation that unveils the purpose of it all, the line to Christ. But what then is the relationship between the Old Testament and other religious history? Is the religious history of others an error and falsehood, and the Old Testament alone revelation? If that be the case, how can God be he who works in all history?

The question has become more pointed since it must now be accepted as established fact that the Old Testament and late Judaism, and through the latter the New Testament and Christianity, had close affinities with the religions of the surrounding world and received strong impulses from them. I am thinking of such central things as dualism (the understanding of good and evil as powers reaching down to the root of existence, dividing it into two sharply separated camps) and the idea that evil is the strongest characteristic of "natural man." We are thinking also of the eschatological attitude and with it the lifting of salvation out of the plane of national politics to that of transcendent universalism, and the ideas of resurrection, the Son of man, and so on. It was primarily Persian influence that was asserting itself here, but also, through it, Babylonian; in the history of Jewish religion these influences sometimes brought in innovations, sometimes merely enhanced native Jewish tendencies.[1] But all these things are sanctioned in the New Testament and form fundamental features in the proclamation of Jesus and the apostles. Is this God's revelation, then, only when it is in Palestine, but not when it was in Persia? Or is it perhaps not revelation at all, but only something that must be peeled off from Christianity?

Here we must hold tight to the fact that the history of revelation and salvation by our principle is all history that God created and guided. Even sin and evil belong to the raw material that must carry out God's plan.

Then we must also humbly see that it is part of God's plan to let evil *run to the end of its tether,* in order that its consequences may be revealed to us (Rom. 1:22-32). This is why peoples, kingdoms, and cultures have gone under. It is also from this point of view that the last saga writer of the Old Testament (the Chronicler) wants the whole history of his people Israel to be seen. And perhaps this is the way in which we ought to look upon the "progress" in Europe and the world at large today. Consequently, good and evil are wrestling with each other in all religions; even in Judaism evil finally triumphed: for example, in its rejection of Christ, or in its own petrification

[1] See G. Hölscher, *Geschichte der Israelitischen und Jüdischen Religion* (Giessen: 1922), pp. 160 ff.

in rabbinism. Seen from one standpoint, history is the story of man's sin and folly, and the history of religions a story of trial and error.

On the other hand, however, it is an undeniable biblical idea that God has also revealed himself outside of the biblical religions, outside of the history of Israel and the Jewish people. The pagans seek an "unknown God" (Acts 17:23), but they *do seek* him and understand that he is different from their own all too human gods. Also the pagans *know* something about God, Paul says; God has revealed himself to them in the order of nature and in the ethical law in their conscience (Rom. 1:18 ff.). In their religions this "natural revelation," as systematic theology has called it, is expressed and it determines the attitude toward that of God which they glimpse.

An even deeper insight into this secret is found in the Gospel of John. The eternal Word of God that became flesh in Christ has been active in the world from the creation of the world (John 1:3), and has also been active in that which men in the earliest stages knew and grasped of God and religious life: "The light shines in the darkness" and "the darkness did not accept it";[2] still "in him was life, and the life was the light of men" (John 1:4)—there were always some who let themselves be more or less enlightened.

Therefore the "apologetes" of the early Church speak of the *logos spermatikos,* the Word in embryonic form, which always and everywhere has been active in the world, and which as budding growth was to be found everywhere that one encountered a true, a "Christian" idea and an approach toward "Christian" living among the gentile thinkers and founders of religion such

[2] The translation of the Norwegian Bible (John 1:5*b*) and used by Mowinckel. (Translator's note)

as Socrates or Plato. Through the Word the real God has been in contact with them, has unveiled something of himself to them.

Hence it is both biblical and "Christian" to acknowledge a divine revelation, a contact with God, a spiritual light, even though broken and unclear, among the great religious heroes of other religions. There have been "prophets" in India, in Persia, in China, and in Greece. There is, therefore, no reason to call Mohammed a deceiver or a false prophet, as one still read in the church history of my school days. If we believe in God, then we must also reckon with the possibility that a man like Mohammed was in contact with this God and that God had something to say to him, a task to give him. I spoke above of the fact that no person can understand and accept more from God than lies within the framework of his own personal and historical (cultural, social, moral) presuppositions.

A man's conception, his appropriation of what God wishes to guide him to see, is always dependent upon the presuppositions of his own time and milieu. Thus also with Mohammed. We cannot, therefore, label him a false prophet but must call him a prophet to a great degree bound and limited by his time. But in faithfulness to historical truth we must add: a prophet whose own ego seems more and more to have influenced how he was led and what he experienced. The border line between the false and the true prophet is in a sense fluctuating—all prophets are selfish, sinful men. In another sense it is as fine as a hair, but it is not given to man to draw that line of distinction.

The revelation of God, then, in its widest sense is not limited to the "Book," any more than his self-giving, re-creating activity ended with apostolic times. Consequently, there is a connection between biblical spiritual history and the religious history of other peoples.

We have seen that the real and essential line of historical revelation runs through Israel. This line, however, goes further back, and side lines come in from other directions. All of this has found its acceptance as a link in the history of divine revelation through becoming a part of the New Testament and as a part of the preaching of Jesus and the apostles. That which God in Jesus Christ has sanctioned and sanctified *is* thereby sanctified; they *are* ideas of revelation. "What God has cleansed, you must not call common." (Acts 10:15.) And as all things were created by and for Christ (Col. 1:16-17), these ideas and foregleams in other religions were, so to speak, created and prepared in history, in order that he might take them up and thereby express his being and his work—in the idea of the "Son of man" still more clearly than in the Jewish idea of the Messiah.

Comparative religion endangers our faith just as little as does the historical view of the Bible.

God's Word—
Concrete and Relevant

43. The *practical problem* when it comes to using the Old Testament as word of God, therefore, is not that revelation is historically conditioned and limited, that it is "broken testimony," closely tied to gentile surroundings and stamped with human incompleteness. It is rather that revelation according to God's own plan and determination is carried on through a historical "process" of divine self-unveiling and self-mediation through what happens—a *history* of revelation and salvation.

The practical problem lies in the fact that the character of Old Testament as testimony *to us,* as word of God *to us,* only partially comes to recognition in us, only partially attests itself as word of God through the Spirit's mediation. Or to express it more simply: if we are honest, we will have to admit that we are able to hear God speaking to us only through parts of the Old Testament, and that we normally feel great sections of it to be irrelevant to us, documents of the past, archaeology, "dust."

Against this experience stands the directive of Scripture itself, "For whatever was written in former days was written *for our instruction,* that by steadfastness and by the encouragement of the scriptures we might have hope" (Rom. 15:4, italics mine). We, therefore, have to ask ourselves the question: How does anything become word of God for us?

44. In order to clarify this matter we will have to take a look at an important side of revelation that is closely connected with its historical character: namely, its *concreteness* and *relevance to a present moment.*

On the basis of the understanding that revelation is something historical, is God's creative, judging, and saving self-mediation in history, light is shed anew upon what every Christian knows by instinct: that God's word is not something abstract, not "eternal truths" in the sense of abstract truths, whether rational or suprarational.

God's word is always something *concrete* and *alive*. Revelation is not information out of the blue of timeless general truths. God makes himself known to one definite man in his definite situation and gives him exactly what his situation demands. Neither is it a revelation of things existentially irrelevant to that man, but rather something that demands his personal answer, demands that he take a position in regard to it. It addresses primarily not his reason, but his conscience and will. It is something that demands that it be given decisive significance for the whole religious, moral, and intellectual existence of that person or his group. It is something existential, a life-or-death challenge. "Thus says the Lord: 'Go and say to. . . . Go and do thus and so!' " "If you are willing and obedient, you shall eat the good of the land; but if you refuse and rebel, you shall be devoured by the sword." (Isa. 1:19 ff.) This is the standing preface and form of the word of revelation in the Old Testament.

It is concrete, bound to a definite time, place, and person—existential. And as creative power, it is also a dynamic thing. This is true even for what seems to have the character of fixed, static truths. If the very heart of the New Testament revelation can be summed up thus: Jesus is the Son of God, the Christ, then this is not a communication that can be filed away, information of only the same value to me as, for instance, the fact that there is a great continent at the South Pole, or that it is so-and-so many million light-years to the Milky Way. It is a communication that demands that I take a position in regard to it. If Jesus Christ is the Son of God, this fact must have consequences for all my living. This demand is latent in the message itself. This concreteness of the revelation is clearest of all in the fact that the Word became flesh. "The Word," without any modifier, is the concrete man Jesus Christ.

45. Another side of the concreteness of revelation is its *relevance* to the present moment. Into one's present situation the concrete word of God comes with its solution to the problem of just that concrete situation.

This is especially clear in the Old Testament, as some examples will show. The ancient Israelites went to the priest to get an oracle from him, for instance, when they did not know who had committed a secret murder or how a difficult case at law should be judged. So they got an "oracle" from Yahweh or his instruction in the law (Torah). In the oldest primitive times the priest "read" the oracle of Yahweh by casting lots or by other mechanical or technical means. As time passed, a fund of such decisions and principles was gathered that could be used as precedents. Guidance was then given by tradition or by deductions from similar cases. The solution might also have come as a thought, an "intuition," perhaps in a dream or a vision. In any case, the answer was given in reference to the case in question as a word of God relevant to a present moment.

A man, for instance, has lost his donkeys and goes to the "seer" in order to have him "see" where they have gone. The seer answers as the situation demands. That the situation has greater depth than the persons in question can see, and that God has a plan that aims further, does not change the matter. The word still has relevance to the moment and does not say more than is *then* necessary. What is to happen later will be seen and understood in due time (I Sam. 9:1–10:7). Another time the king and his chieftains are about to fortify the city against a hostile attack and are inspecting the dams and the conduits. Then the prophet comes with the word from God that the situation of the moment demands (Isa. 7). Again, the people are celebrating a cultic festival with pomp and circumstance; suddenly the prophet stands in their midst with the word of doom from the Lord that says what he thinks about such worship and what true worship is (Amos). Or some women come, carefree and happy, from the Temple feast and the cultic dance; the prophet meets them with the word that foretells that before the year is out the City and the Temple will be lying desolate (Isa. 32:9 ff.). Or the leaders of the people who remained in Judah after the deportation come to Jeremiah and ask him to tell them the will of God, whether they are to flee to Egypt or remain in the country. After he has listened ten days for it, "the word of the Lord [comes] to Jeremiah," and its tenor is that they shall remain (Jer. 42).

It is the same in the New Testament.[1] The disciples ask Jesus to teach them to pray, and he gives them the Lord's Prayer. A rich young man comes to Jesus distressed about the salvation of his soul; then Jesus points out what is of present importance to *him,* his wealth and his reliance upon it, and proclaims that Word of God that for all its concreteness is still the principle for solving *that* problem wherever it occurs. Or take the case of Paul. He hears of conditions in some church or knows out of personal experience where they need guidance. So he sends them the inspired letters that say what had to be said just *then* about the difficulties of *that* time.

In reality it is this relevance of the Word to a particular present that makes it the Word of God to *us* also. It is one thing for God's word to be word of God *per se* and quite another for it to become God's word *to us, to me.* If the Word had eternally remained "with God," then it would have been without effect or significance for man. Then it would not have been "God's word," that is, not his *revealed* word. This was the very reason that "the Word became flesh and dwelt amongst us." This incarnation is repeated every day. The fact that there exists a word of God *per se* as a revealed book between two covers has not *per se* the least significance for me if it does not become present reality to me. If it does not, then it is as Isaiah says: "The vision of all this has become to you like the words of a book that is sealed. When men give it to one who can read, saying, 'Read this,' he says, 'I cannot, for it is sealed.' And when they give the book to one who cannot read, saying, 'Read this,' he says, 'I cannot read.' " (Isa. 29:11-12.) Something additional must come to open that word to me.

[1] For the following I am indebted to Ragnar Asting, *Die Verkündigung des Wortes im Urchristentum* (Stuttgart, 1939), pp. 458 ff.

Let us here be realistic and not create for ourselves soporific and sedative illusions like certain Barthians who dream about automatically effective "preaching." In the situation of present-day man it has little or no effect to show a man in spiritual (often still unconscious) distress that the word of God can be found in the Bible; if he will only accept it; for to his distress, objectively seen, often belongs the fact that he does not believe that there is a God and consequently neither does he accept any such thing as "word of God." The Bible to him is, at the most, an interesting cultural document of the human mind, a testimony to mankind's most beautiful and tragic illusion. Secondly, the word in the Bible exists as that which was pertinent to a vanished past, and consequently often speaks in a form that makes it impossible for the uninitiated to discover that it has any present relevance for him. One may, upon authority, take over the conviction or the opinion that it is word of God—only it has no significance whatever if it does not become more than mere opinion accepted on authority. God's word becomes *relevant for me* when it (that is, a very specific detail in it) hits me in a tender spot, strikes into my situation, and smites my conscience. Not until then does it become word of God to me. That is: then it begins to make God's word a judging and saving action upon me, and by that I sooner or later realize that it is God's word.

This possibility depends upon two things. First, upon the "objective" fact that God's word really *is* "like fire, . . . like a hammer which breaks the rock in pieces" (Jer. 23:29); that it is "living and active, sharper than any two-edged sword, piercing to the division of soul and spirit, of joints and marrow, and discerning the thoughts and intentions of the heart" (Heb. 4:12). Secondly, it is dependent upon the fact that it can come to me in a form that makes me recognize my own present situation in that situation for which the specific word was once formed, so that the gap of some thousands of intervening years is immediately bridged. In short, the word is made alive as that which it is, a testimony, by being testified as actual testimony by one who experienced it as true and, therefore, personally guarantees it.

Then the word becomes to me what the Barthians call *existential* (the expression originated with Kierkegaard): relevant for me and intervening in my life with re-creative power.

Basically the power of God's own Spirit is in the word, and this Spirit begins to work within me, opening my eyes, causing me to see my own situation as it is exposed by the word. It is the Spirit that according to the promise of Christ is "witnessing," that is, is creating an entrance for Christ. This is the "testimony of the Spirit together with our spirit," or in the term of old theologians: *"testimonium spiritus sancti,"* which first makes clear to me that the word of God really is word of God.

46. Here again we meet the problem that we encountered above, for it becomes clear that the Old Testament does not hit each one of us as a homogeneous word of God. Neither does it hit all in the same way. Only single passages, chapters, or verses impress themselves upon us as words of God, thereby becoming God's word to us. There is much in the Old Testament that seems to us to be dead stuff, and for many present-day Christians there certainly is much in the Old Testament that will forever remain so.

This problem in reality is the same for the fundamentalist with his dogma of verbal plenary inspiration as for the realist with a historical view of the Bible. The fundamentalist, however, seems to have an apparent help in his scriptural dogma. It gives him absolution beforehand for any arbitrary reinterpretation of the present text and for any artificial attempt to find his own time described in the words. The realist here will feel with double strength his distance from certain things, for instance: the glowing prayers for revenge in the Old Testament, the blood-dripping sacrificial cultus, and the wilderness of regulations about cleanness and uncleanness. He will have difficulties with the rules for which types of food may be eaten and which are taboo with the whole ritualism and observance of Judaism, even within the Old Testament. We may very well understand, just because we look upon it all historically, that in the situation of that time the word of God had to come in such a way, with such forms of worship, discipline, will to sacrifice, responsibility, and surrender as we meet there. But can that have any bearing whatever upon our lives today?

This question cannot be solved by a simple formula. We can only say that here too Christian life itself will give us some viewpoints.

First of all, I mention *Christian fellowship.* The experience of the individual is only a link in the total experience of the Church. As a Christian I participate in this; as a Christian I am not 4 or 40 years old but 1,958 years old; and if we take the Church as a whole, there possibly is no word in the Old Testament that at some time or another has not been word of God to someone. In this multiplicity we see the wealth of God's providence. There is always something for everyone. Anybody can find that which he needs in his situation. It may not even be God's will that all should need or use everything.

Secondly, there is a *task* here. The Spirit of God is to guide us into all truth, but there were some things the disciples were not yet able to bear (John 16:12-13). Development, growth in knowledge, understanding and receptivity, willingness and dedication, here are presupposed as normal. The task is to be willing to read and listen, to ask and let God speak.

Thirdly, there is here a *special task for theology* and for preachers and teachers well versed in the Scriptures, for it is through the most thorough historical study of the Scriptures and the best possible penetration into the time in which "the word of God came" (John 10:35) that it will be made easier to find the analogies to our personal and historical situation and thereby make the Scriptures speak to us.

Let me, for example, again mention the intense prayers in the book of Psalms for revenge upon one's "enemies" and for their death. When we realize that these often are not the personal or national enemies of the worshiper, but "evil spirits" and "uncanny powers" that the worshiper sees as causes for his misfortune, then the bridge is laid for a Christian use of these texts, for I know my "evil spirits" even if I do not today conceive of them as "materialized" as they did at that time. They are called Dishonesty, Impurity, Selfishness, Lovelessness, Fear, Bitterness, Hatred, and the like; and my misfortune (and ours) is that we, like the demoniac in Mark 5, identify ourselves with our evil spirits. We *want* them and cater to them, suffer under them and curse them; but at the bottom of our souls we *do not want* to get rid of them. The way to get rid of them, however, is to confess them, call them by name, learn to hate them and to deny ourselves in them, ask God to break them and us in them, and constantly watch and pray that they do not return when Jesus Christ has driven them out. We ourselves are "our enemies," and against these enemies there also exists a Christian "prayer of revenge."

Revelation as Testimony and Sharing

47. It was mentioned above (45) that one of the necessary conditions, if the word is to strike me and become existential for me, is that it be presented by someone who guarantees it. This testimony of the witness is extremely important, for he testifies unreservedly how the word struck him and at what concrete point it struck. It is in fact *there* that the word of God is transcribed into relevant form: the testimony form. Indeed one can say that the testimony *is* word of God to him whom it strikes, brings to his senses, and leads to conversion and salvation. Then God's Spirit is truly testifying together with the spirit of the person who is proclaiming and testifying.

The truth of this is connected with a matter that also has been touched above—that God's *word* itself really is testimony.

It is testimony in a double sense—as *God's testimony about himself* and as *man's inspired testimony about God.*

God's revelation as activity in history is testimony concerning himself, his being, plan, and salvation. This testimony really is not limited to the Book (see Rom. 1:19-20; Acts 14:17), but in the Book it is seen most clearly.

This self-testimony of God is also involved in the testimony of his inspired witnesses. That is what the revelatory writings of the Book are: testimony! God's word and revelation have come to us altogether in the form of testimony.

"Testimony" in the biblical sense is simultaneously both proclamation and witnessing—proclamation that testifies and testimony that proclaims. "To testify" is in the biblical sense no neutral act: it means to stake one's life for another, not for something but for someone, not for an idea or a cause but for a person. In the Old Testament the same verb, *he'id,* means both "testify" and "solemnly affirm, declare, enforce, warn, mention as example"; and the cognate noun *'eduth* means both "testimony" and "a solemnly given and received ordinance and exhortation," and is used especially of the revealed law of God, both the Ten Commandments and the Law of Moses. Another word of the same root, *the'udah,* is also used of the preaching of the prophets, together with the word *torah* that ordinarily denotes the "law" but really means "(divine) guidance" through priest or prophet (Isa. 8:16). God attests himself through his word, and those to whom "the word of God has come" (that is, to whom it has become active reality) "testify" about God and his nature and will and what they have experienced of it.

The view of the New Testament is similar to this. When God testifies, he reveals his will and plan in deed. A witness for God is one who sets forth God's will and who struggles for God's revelation in the world. When Jesus is called "the faithful witness," this means that he is one who does not fail but fights even unto death for God's will and plan. But naturally "witness" also means the eyewitness who testifies to what he has seen and experienced (I John 1). In the union of these two elements lies the testimonial character of revelation.

The disciples received the task of being witnesses in this sense as a commission from Jesus (John 15:27). By carrying it out, they continue the work of Jesus; and for this task they receive the power of the Holy Spirit. It belongs to the nature of their testimony that God or Christ is working through it. It is creative, in the first place, in the sense that it pushes men into decision and demands an answer. It confronts them with the consequences, that is, the decision as to whether they will accept the grace of God or not. It is creative, in the second place, by producing new life in those who answer "yes." A "witness" in the fullest sense is he who becomes one with Christ, surrenders completely to him, gives him his full will and love, and has received his Spirit and lets his life be led by him. He, therefore, also becomes one with his suffering and his Cross. This is the highest form of Christian testimony. It is Christ, God in Christ, who is both the content and the motive power in the testimony.

It is in this sense that revelation and the books of revelation, including the Old Testament, are testimony. It is God's own testimony and the inspired testimony of his witnesses. Thereby it is the judging and restoring testimony that confronts us, one by one, with the choice, the decision.

It is this testimonial character of the Old Testament that must be made vivid and set in motion, as it were. It takes place precisely through him who identifies himself with it, who has experienced that God encountered him through it, and who, therefore, can testify that in this way it became God's word to him. This is as self-evident as the New Testament idea that a witness in the fullest sense is he who is one with Christ.

48. The task both for theology and for the practical devotional use of scripture is to take this seriously. It is necessary to conquer the distance of time and to become *contemporary* with the witnesses. We have to get on an even footing with the prophets, the poets of the psalms, the tellers of saga, and the givers of law, so we can *share their experiences of God.*

A choice example of such sharing with us is furnished in the Bible itself by *Jeremiah.* Not a few of the prophetic words that he was inspired to have recorded after twenty-two years of work are prayers and outbursts of his heart to God and the answers God gave him.[1] They are concerned with his prophetic calling and with the attitude of the people toward his preaching. In this way they belong to the general public. But they are primarily concerned with his personal problems and difficulties. Since in spite of this he included them (perhaps without himself knowing why), it was because he was led to reveal all that bears upon his relationship to God. He includes even those prayers and laments that were not answered: they all belong to the revelation of how God worked with this man and how he reacted to God's demands and testings. In his confession of "ignoble" thoughts and wishes there lies a part of his rendering account of himself to God—what Jeremiah must accept in order to continue to be "the mouthpiece of God." He shared this with us so we may know what sort of material God can work with and use when he gets it melted and purified and may learn from Jeremiah how to render honest account of ourselves, confess our sins, and share our experiences.

This is a matter that imposes a double task. The task for theology is to work out and draw up the clearest possible picture of the historical situation and the outward and inward, per-

[1] Jer. 11:18-23; 12:1-6; 15:10-21; 17:12-18; 18:18-23; 20:7-13; 20:14-18. Cf. the word to Baruch, ch. 45.

sonal and general, circumstances that have influenced each of the Old Testament writings and sayings. In addition to this, the task is to "transpose" all this for our own situation, to point out that which is universal in it and has special analogies with our present situation, both as individuals and as a society. What, for instance, is the deepest similarity between the moral and social situation of the prophets and our own? What is universal in the situation of those listening to the prophets, and how does this express itself today? What is it that this prophet or that composer of psalms really experienced, and how did this influence what he says? Further, does it point to a need within us? How can what the prophets say prepare the way for a similar experience in us?

A fruitful sharing, however, also demands that each one make himself contemporary with the past and ask: What does this say to me *today?* With this word what does God want of me today? What does it make me see within myself that God wants changed? Of God's will and plan of salvation what does it let me see that has bearing upon me and my need, my task and my earthly vocation? Every moment of each man's life is a situation of decision. The important thing is to let God speak and then to let his speaking settle the matter.

All this should cast some light upon the problem of the "dead matter" in the Old Testament. It is the task both of the theologian and of the individual to get it to speak by our getting to be on speaking terms with it ourselves. I speak to the word, and it speaks to me, so that more and more of it can open itself to me. This is an unending task, both for each individual and for theology.

Was Christum Treibet

49. It seems appropriate here to say something also about the aim of this work from the standpoint of content.

The simplest and most important statement on the subject was made by Luther in his well-known principle for the interpretation of the Old Testament: what one must find is *was Christum treibet.* This is an expression from everyday speech. The German word *treiben* is of the same linguistic root as English "drive," and as an American can say "to drive a truck," a German can attach his verb to any sort of occupation—farming, studies, and so on—thereby indicating the pursuit of an activity toward a goal. It thus means "to work with and obtain results from," "to work (something) forward." What we must do, then, in our practical use of the Bible is to get hold of that testimony that "impels toward Christ," that makes Christ the goal of its activity.

Here it might be appropriate to say a few words about the theological, more theoretical side of the problem, which was already touched upon in paragraphs 14 and 15. What is necessary to say here can shortly be expressed in this way: The divinely guided history of culture and religion which the Old Testament places before us reaches its goal in Jesus Christ. This is true not only of the nonreflective emphasis which Jesus and the apostles laid upon the prophecies and the Old Testament institutions (such as the sacrifice) as symbols pointing forward to the realization in Christ. It is true also, and to a more organically coherent degree, of the history revealed to us by a critical scientific interpretation of the sources (compare above, paragraph 20). The very line in the historical development as it is represented by the laws, the psalms, the prophets, and the eschatological hope leads as its "legitimate" historical result forward to Jesus from Nazareth.

We can say that from a strictly historical viewpoint the "line of development" begins to divide itself after the consolidation of the Jewish congregation in postexilic time. The one is represented by the steadily tighter realization of the supremacy of the law forward to the rabbinic and pharisaic religion of law. The other is represented by the ever-rising emphasis laid upon the universalistic, the personal, the otherworldly, the "messianism," as the hope of a savior in the noblest sense of that word. It is this line which reaches its climax in Jesus Christ.

From a Christian standpoint there can be no doubt which of these lines is the "legitimate" one. One might sum it up in this way: What the historical development in the Old Testament had prepared and what its inspired men looked forward to, longed and hoped for, that God made reality in Jesus Christ. He made it real in a way which supercedes all expectation, hope, and prophecy in the Old Testament.

This is really also the basic viewpoint which Jesus himself and the early Christian Church had of the history of revelation in the Old Testament. Only they did not express themselves in such theological categories. Neither did they have the same understanding of the singular points of this history —an understanding which present-day critical historical investigation has made possible. Neither did they meditate upon the connection between this "sacred history" and secular history.

To the earliest Christians the prophecies played an important part, as they looked at the relationship between the Old Testament and the fulfillment in Christ. This, however, does not mean that when it comes to our religious use of the Old Testament, we primarily should look for as many detailed "messianic prophecies" as possible. It means rather that we shall look for the major lines [1] and try to understand how the goal of Old Testament history is reached in Christ, and that it is a fulfillment, a realization, which goes far beyond anything the inspired men of the Old Testament could grasp. The proposition that the Old Testament says *what* Christ is, the New Testament *who* he is,[2] simply is not correct. It can be maintained only by an arbitrary allegorical interpretation that reads the whole New Testament into the Old, thereby violating both the text and the biblical ideas concerning revelation as a certain history—an idea that the Old Testament expressly wants to stress by rendering the history of Israel as a history of divinely guided education. The fact that the New Testament lays great weight upon the proof of Christ from prediction gives us no right to expect or demand that

[1] Cf. C. H. Dodd, *According to the Scriptures* (New York: Charles Scribner's Sons, 1953).

[2] W. Vischer, *The Witness of the Old Testament to Christ* (London: Lutterworth Press, 1947), I, 7.

more or less every chapter and verse of the Old Testament shall contain predictions of Christ.[3] The idea of the New Testament as "fulfillment," that is, the actual completion and realization of the goal toward which the historical revelation of the Old Testament steered, cannot be employed as a method of interpretation or an exegetical master key that would more or less force one to find Christological statements everywhere in it. In addition, the Old Testament testimony to Christ is "broken testimony," expressing what believers were then able to conceive of the promises of God, clothed as they were in an imperfection conditioned by time and circumstances: inklings of truth and expectations of sheer faith that point forward to a completion. Most of the "messianic" expectations in the Old Testament are on a level so far below the fulfillment in Christ that they can only throw an indirect light upon Christ. They show, for instance, the hard material that God has to handle in us, what it costs him to break loose from our individual, national, and racial selfishness, for that inborn will to limit the benefits of salvation to one's own society is by nature basically the same for Aryan and Jew. It is tragicomic that the mentality and morality most fiercely attacking what is Jewish in the Old Testament is a particularistic racial pride of exactly the same nature as the "Jewishness" against which it is fighting. It is basically the "Jew," that is, the natural, unconverted, thoroughly selfish man within the "Aryan," who is rising up against the humanity, the universality, that is in Christ.

But if the "messianic" sayings in the Old Testament are able to unveil and judge our human nature, they also unveil to us our actual yearning for salvation and for a helper, a yearning

[3] Dodd, *op. cit.*

that also belongs to our human existence—an inkling of our need for one who is higher, nobler, purer, closer to God, than we. And inasmuch as the "Word" expressed itself in the Old Testament terms for these needs and inklings, these, too, have become God's speaking to us, pointing forward to the real fulfillment of the needs, the real Savior.

In the very light of the imperfection in the Old Testament's messianic expectations, what Christ is (the real Christ Jesus) emerges all the more clearly for us. Because of this we obtain the right to read the expectations—the broken testimony concerning God's earlier promises in this history of education—in the light of their fulfillment and to see the unity of the divine revelation in the two Testaments.

The Old Testament in Paul's judgment is a "tutor unto Christ. According to Paul's insight, to "impel toward Christ" by the use of the Old Testament, therefore, probably means first of all to direct my eye toward that which can *impel me to Christ,* see *my* sin, and *my* coresponsibility for the sin in the society of which I am a part—and in interaction with this impel me also to see God's demand, and from the sight of both to look toward Christ.

God's demand!—his loftiness and *holiness,* his world-embracing plan, and the connection between his own holiness and the absolute obligatoriness ("holiness") of his "law." These things shine forth more clearly in the Old Testament, it may be, than anywhere else in the Bible. "You shall be holy, for I the Lord, your God, am holy." This command here receives a concrete form that is naturally characterized by the situations, tasks, and ideas of the past, but in its basic demand and in its urge to be concrete it challenges and obligates us today. But in doing so, it awakens our acknowledgment of sin and impels us to Christ and the grace of God.

In this connection I would like once more to refer to the subject of "clean" and "unclean" animals. I mentioned above that the conception of "cleanness" in the Old Testament was wholly characterized by the primitive view that it is especially the outward things and one's association with them that makes a man unclean. This uncleanness is a sort of contagious matter coming from certain animals and things that makes a man "taboo" in the negative sense: brings misfortune to the man in question, ruins his "power of soul" and his success (his "blessing," as ancient Israel called it), and thereby also ruins his "uprightness," his ability to do for himself and his own what was both morally and practically right. It is this same external magical view of cleanness that leads to such consequences as the caste system in India. There certain classes of men are "unclean" simply because they belong to this class or that. It is this externalism with which Jesus manifestly breaks when he says, "Not what goes into the mouth defiles a man, but what comes out of the mouth, this defiles a man" (Matt. 15:11). "For out of the heart come evil thoughts, murder, adultery, fornication, theft, false witness, slander. These are what defile a man." (Matt. 15:19-20.) But the subject "clean and unclean" still can teach even us, who can build upon Jesus' moral conception of uncleanness, how necessary it is to take the demand of cleanness seriously instead of making it a hazy ideal with no bearing upon daily living. The question of cleanness presents itself a hundred times a day with constant proddings toward sin in thought, word, and deed. The demand, therefore, must be concrete, not a form of juridical casuistry, if we are to apply it in actual life and thereby fulfill it. It is necessary for us to see the hundreds of possibilities in order to fulfill the ideal of cleanness and avoid impurity; for even though the latter comes from the heart, it is naturally helped and strengthened by external things. The topic of "clean and unclean" in the Old Testament teaches us exactly this necessity for concretizing the ideal of purity in our daily life, in our relationship to animals and things and men. Our danger is not with animals not chewing the cud nor with fish not having "fins and scales." Rather, it is found in books, pictures, social customs, jargon, our own laziness and lack of discipline, our false ideas of liberty, our stupid sensational interest in the latest "science," our fear of not being modern, and so on and so forth, and last but not least our perennial urge to haggle with God and to drive as close to the ditch as possible. It may be well worth mentioning here—and we may say so without exaggerating—that it is this serious view of "holiness" and "cleanness" in the Old Testament—even though the terms originally were not ethically oriented—that through Christianity led to the development of that sexual morality which laid the foundations to the spiritual welfare of the Western world.

My purpose here is not to point out all the spheres in which the Old Testament has a special message to us that directly or indirectly prepares the way for Christ. Only a few examples must suffice.

Fellowship and *common responsibility* have been uniquely set forth in a study of Israel's view of the "tribe" and the "covenant" by Professor Johannes Pedersen in his book *Israel.* Hardly anything could give us a clearer picture of truly "ideal" fellowship, with its responsibility and duty, willingness and love, as the Old Testament sees it. His book is a course in social attitudes needed by us. Let us think for a moment of the possibilities latent in a mode of thinking that uses the very same word for "right," "duty," and "custom." There is no "right" that is not at the same time duty; and both of them are hollow if they do not also come to be our custom, our normal way of action—for the word means *this* too!

What primitive Israel has to tell us is completed by the prophets. They work with all their might to keep the demand for love from being rejected—that active feeling of fellowship (*hesed*) and "righteousness," which also includes the will and the ability to maintain that fellowship by being righteous oneself—even when society grows big and complicated, demanding new social structures and placing new and unexpected demands socially, administratively, and juridically. This is exactly what had taken place in Israel. The transition to new cultural forms with fixed dwelling places, farming, business, and money economy had crushed the ancient social units and was in the process of destroying both "fellowship" and "righteousness" in the sense of a man's duty to uphold his "fellow covenanter."

Isn't this exactly (albeit in different forms) the situation of our time? In our capitalistic society with its laissez-faire competition we are at the end of our rope, and we see that the result is dissolution of all ethical standards: man as naked ego has come out into the open. Besides, we find great masses of people becoming aware of the necessity of a thoroughgoing change and thinking that they have the program for it, but who are beginning to realize that programs are not enough. What is needed is a presupposition inside of man himself, an ethical foundation; this cannot be built upon ego, nor upon the expanded ego of a class, but only upon such "old-fashioned" ideas as "inner freedom" and "good will."

The prophets see clearly that such a fellowship as they are trying to restore is wholly dependent upon its being anchored in something higher and more absolute, something of a completely different nature from both ego and "my group" (my people, my class). It must be anchored in God and connected with the will to "know God," listen to him, surrender to his guidance in all things great or small. This is so even in politics! Even in the question of war and peace! Even in the question of poverty and wealth! Even in the problem of ways to solve these problems. Nothing less than God's dominion, God's reign, will do.

Our thoughts then go directly to the questions: How shall we attain this? Where shall we find the power for such reconstruction? Who was it who said: "Whatever you wish that men would do to you, do so to them" (Matt. 7:12)? Hasn't all our history shown that we cannot do it? But did he not also say: "With God nothing will be impossible"? And "Come to me all who labor and are heavy-laden, and I will give you rest"? The way to God leads through acknowledgment of sin and God's grace in Jesus Christ. Christ's power alone can lay the foundation for the new society. He it is, therefore, who continues the line from the prophets and points the way to a society, a fellowship, much more radical and effective than any of our earthly programs—if we are only willing to take it seriously!

Unsparingly the prophets unveil what it is in the individual and the community (and in me!)—that hinders such a fellowship and delays the reign of God: lust, greed, selfishness, disobedience, pride, contentiousness, vanity, fear, hatred. Nor do they spare "piety," with its inherited forms and customs, that is, the selfishness, unwillingness, and indifference that so often hide behind it, often unconsciously. Amos has a sentence about the holy places of his time and its inherited services and all that its antiquity-flavored piety regarded as a holy legacy from the patriarchs. His sentence is so sharp and even crude that in modern language it has to be translated: "To hell with the churches and the organizations if there can be no righteousness, honesty, and goodness in the land!" (Amos 4:4; 5:5, 21-22). All the other prophets of doom say the same.

The truly pious ones in the Old Testament more and more understand that evil is not located in conditions and circumstances, in "society" and "milieu." Its location is in ourselves. "Break up your fallow ground, and sow not among thorns. Circumcise yourselves to the Lord" (Jer. 4:3-4.) It is located too deep, however, to be removed by outward means. Whatever may be the origin of evil, it has become our nature (Jer. 13:23).

Thus they are driven out beyond themselves, beyond that which is "natural" and "possible." God himself must intervene and re-create, give a "heart of flesh instead of a heart of stone," give a new spirit, write the "law" in their hearts rather than on stone tablets and in books. But how can this take place? Can an ideal king, a new David, do it? Perhaps it can happen if one who is really "righteous" in the full meaning of that word voluntarily intercedes for those who are not, takes upon himself the burden of all the evil they have caused, identifies himself with them, sees their sin as *his* responsibility and his sin, and accepts his sufferings as punishment for *this* failure of responsibility. Does such a righteous one exist? Is the suffering servant of the Lord described in Isa. 53 an "ideal figure" or a real person? It is an old question of interpretation: "About whom . . . does the prophet say this, about himself or about some one else?" (Acts 8:34). Maybe this righteous servant already lives unknown and misunderstood. Perhaps he is now atoning without our knowing it? Is there one who will represent the whole of mankind in this way? Does there exist and will there sometime come a "Son of man" such as the Zoroastrians talk about—a new Adam, a father for a re-created mankind? What is demanded of Israel, of each one of us, in order that he may come?

These are the questions asked between the lines in the Old Testament and the Apocrypha. However, also in the Old Testament, God's absolute love is the first and last word—as expressed in the election, in the Covenant, in the conviction that God himself will do it! (Cf. paragraph 28.)

Phylogenesis and ontogenesis are parallel, the biologists say: the individual repeats the development of the race. Old Testament history led the race of man forward to the place where it could meet Christ. It can lead us, individually, there today. Every day we need to be led to that place one by one, all the more now that we are Christians.

What we have seen and received as Christians, however, also reflects light upon the Old Testament, so that we now can see the full implication of that which then was more in the nature of inklings, dreams, and longings. Its words, therefore, now can speak directly to us about Christ, about that which we have received from him, about the high goal, the great responsibility, the glorious salvation and help, and the shining hope that we have in him. They can, therefore, place before us every day choice and decision, causing us to surrender to him who wants us and can use us in spite of our absolute nothingness and uselessness.

50. To sum it all up: The question was raised, How can we differentiate between God's word and human words in the Old Testament when revelation is in history itself, when divine words and human words lie interwoven in an indissoluble unity, and when no mechanical distinction is possible and no infallible key can be recommended? How can we solve the problem that the Old Testament only in parts validates itself to the individual as Word of God? The answer is found in that surrender to God and in that *unity with Christ* that lets his Spirit work and testify through me. It is also found in the *willingness* to let God speak *to me* through the inspired human testimonies in the Old Testament.

This answer presupposes the honest will to face reality squarely and to take the Old Testament as the historical entity it is without reinterpreting it through self-made theological theories, however venerable they may be, but to give right of way to historical inquiry seeking the truth.

First and last, however, a *praying and listening attitude* is needed—a willingness to let God tell *me* today what *I* need here and now.